THE ART OF SATIRE
Painters as Caricaturists and Cartoonists from Delacroix to Picasso
ぞ

THE ART OF SATIRE
Painters as Caricaturists and Cartoonists from Delacroix to Picasso

by Ralph E. Shikes and Steven Heller

Pratt Graphics Center
and
Horizon Press

FOR RUTH AND LOUISE

COPYRIGHT © 1984 BY RALPH E. SHIKES
AND STEVEN HELLER
Library of Congress Cataloging in
Publication Data

Shikes, Ralph E.
  The art of satire.

  Bibliography: p. 119
  Includes index.
  1. Caricatures and cartoons.   2. Wit and
humor, Pictorial — History — 19th century.
3. Wit and humor, Pictorial — History —
20th century.   I. Heller, Steven.
II. Title.
NC1350.S54   1984   741.5'9'09034   84-650
ISBN 0-8180-0141-0
ISBN 0-8180-0142-9 (pbk.)
Designed by Steven Heller
MANUFACTURED IN THE UNITED STATES
OF AMERICA

Contents

- 7 Acknowledgements
- 8 Painters as Caricaturists and Cartoonists
- 17 Eugène Delacroix
- 20 Pierre Cécile Puvis de Chavannes
- 24 Camille Pissarro
- 26 Edouard Manet
- 28 Claude Monet
- 31 Paul Gauguin
- 34 Jean-Louis Forain
- 37 Maximilien Luce
- 40 Louis Anquetin
- 42 Paul Signac
- 45 Henri de Toulouse-Lautrec
- 48 Félix Vallotton
- 52 Frantisek Kupka
- 55 Jacques Villon
- 58 Kees van Dongen
- 60 Louis Marcoussis
- 63 Pablo Picasso
- 68 Juan Gris
- 72 Sir Edwin Landseer
- 74 Dante Gabriel Rossetti
- 76 Sir John Everett Millais
- 78 Sir Edward Burne-Jones
- 80 James Jacques Joseph Tissot
- 82 Walter Crane
- 86 Walter Richard Sickert
- 88 Lyonel Feininger
- 94 Pascin
- 96 George Grosz
- 101 John Sloan
- 104 George Bellows
- 107 Stuart Davis
- 110 Reginald Marsh
- 112 Ben Shahn
- 114 Ad Reinhardt
- 119 Bibliographies
- 124 Index

Acknowledgements

We would like to express our gratitude to the many in France who made suggestions, steered us to sources, gave us permissions: to Michel Melot, formerly of the Cabinet des Estampes, Bibliothèque Nationale; Mme Denise Fauvel-Rouif of the Institut Français d'Histoire Sociale; the staffs of the Bibliothèque d'Art et d'Archéologie and the Galerie Louise Leiris; the caricaturists Tim, Gus and Ronald Searle; and, especially, Mme Aline Dardel for invaluable help in numerous corners of research.

In England, Sarah Winbush of the National Portrait Gallery was unfailingly patient in responding to numerous inquiries, Sir Ralph R. Millais was gracious in his loans, and the staffs of the William Morris Gallery, the Birmingham Museums and Art Gallery, the London Borough of Islington Library, the British Museum, the Royal Library at Windsor Castle were most helpful in the location of photographs.

We are grateful for suggestions made by Robert Rainwater of the New York Public Library, Riva Castleman of the Museum of Modern Art, Eleanor Garvey of the Houghton Library, Harvard University, and for loans of photos and materials for the exhibition from Marcelle Mabille, Olive Burden, Draper Hill, Seymour Hacker, Earl Davis, Mrs. Anthony J. Garner, and Jacob and Frances Landau. Mr. and Mrs. Herbert D. Schimmel permitted us to photograph from their extensive files of *fin-de-siècle* magazines and to lend us originals from their collection, and Ben Goldstein lent us many drawings from his large files of *The Masses*. Inez Garson in New York and Elaine Senigallia in Rome were very helpful in research. We are grateful to VAGA/S.P.A.D.E.M. for their cooperation, to Andrew Stasik and staff at Pratt Graphics Center for their help in rounding up originals and to Ben Raeburn for his editing. We are especially indebted to Ruth Shikes for invaluable editorial help.

We would also like to thank Jeannie Friedman for her work on the mechanicals, and Janet Seddon and Jesse Mittleman at National Photocomposition Services, Inc., for the care and concern in typesetting this manuscript.

Thanks, also, to the Swann Foundation for Caricature and Cartoon for their invaluable support for this project.

The translation of phrases from Picasso's "The Dream and Lie of Franco," on page 65, is from Alfred H. Barr, Jr.'s *Picasso: Fifty Years of His Art*, published by the Museum of Modern Art.

Painters as Caricaturists and Cartoonists

PAINTERS AS CARICATURISTS AND CARTOONISTS did not topple tyrants, but, like all good satirists, they stirred consciences and fanned the flames of discontent, and they portrayed a comedy of manners, titillating and amusing the populace.

This is a selection of nineteenth- and twentieth-century painters from France, England, Germany and the United States, most of whom worked professionally as caricaturists and cartoonists for scores of satiric periodicals. Also included are painters who were "Sunday caricaturists," primarily dabblers in this genre, who played with the form — sometimes inspiredly — with no intention to publish.

What is meant by "satire," "caricature," "cartoon"? The terms are flexible; the genre is broadly based both in style and content. Included here are examples of satire in two contexts: one that is light, often personal, sometimes self-ridiculing; another that is more serious, satire following the dictionary definition — "trenchant wit, irony, or sarcasm used to expose and discredit vice or folly."

Caricature and cartoon take many forms: personal caricature (Picasso's drawings of his friends, p. 65, for example); political caricature (Tissot's "Napoleon III," p. 81); situation caricature (Sloan's "Circumstances Alter Cases," p. 101); political cartoon (Kupka's "Liberté," p. 53); *portrait charge* (Manet's "Emile Olivier," p. 26); comedy of manners (Forain's untitled drawing, p. 36); captioned cartoon (Reginald Marsh's "Long Island Nights," p. 111); comic strip (Feininger's "Wee Willie Winkies World," p. 90). They deal with many subjects, including overt political issues — war, peace, militarism, colonialism, religion, the judiciary — as well as light social themes. Some of the drawings in this collection have more than one element; some graphic commentaries elude classification.

The painters as caricaturists-cartoonists presented here differ in styles and techniques as much as they do in subject and motivation:

¶ Delacroix, chafing at the stylistic restrictions of the Ecole des Beaux-Arts, copies 40 of Rowlandson's drawings and makes his own political cartoons for *Le Miroir*, raising his voice for freedom long before he painted "Liberty Leading the People";

¶ Dante Gabriel Rossetti, amused by William Morris's hyperintellectuality, pokes fun at Morris's indifference to his beautiful wife;

¶ Monet, at 16, draws caricatures for 20 francs each and earns more money than he was to make as a painter at 26;

¶ Jacques Villon supports himself by satirizing, in beautiful line, French upper-class women;

¶ Gauguin, in Tahiti, avenges himself by caricaturing the colonial officials who had refused him a job he wanted;

¶ Franz Kupka assails capitalism with harsh image and strong line;

¶ Toulouse-Lautrec turns the Judgment of Paris into a sardonic joke;

¶ Louis Marcoussis departs from his political caricatures to draw a classic "he-she" cartoon that college humor magazines have been copying for generations;

¶ George Grosz dips pen in vitriol to caricature the exploiters and the pathological aspects of Weimar society;

¶ Reginald Marsh, in *The New Yorker*, assails lynching in a drawing almost worthy of Daumier.

The periodicals in which their graphics appeared provided training in draftsmanship for many of the artists who were eventually to secure a foothold as painters. As their individual styles developed, their names became known to their readers. Jacques Villon recalled his early days as a cartoonist at the turn of the century: "At that time, the influence of the press on art was incontestable. It helped to speed up the liberation of painting from academicians . . . and let's make it clear that the press of those days just doesn't compare with today's newspapers. The press had a most advanced spirit and the cartoons were done with love, and not just dished out as today."[1]

Villon was exaggerating only slightly when he observed that caricature and cartoon "helped to speed up the liberation of painting from academicians." The exuberance, the lack of academic restraints, the untrammeled approach, and above all the distortions and the exaggerated line — all were elements of uninhibited expression that eventually carried over onto the easel, certainly a factor in the experimentations of Kupka, Villon and Gris, for example. Caricature undoubtedly contributed to an atmosphere that made possible a breakaway from convention and from the rigid rules of academic drawing. In France, it was an effective antidote to the idealization of beauty that prevailed in Salon circles. It may have contributed to German Expressionism, and it became part of the vocabulary of Pop Art in America.

Did the journalistic work of these artists contribute stylistically to their development as painters? In the general sense that caricature helped break the bonds of academic strictures, the answer is yes; in specific terms, very little. The idiosyncratic features of Feininger's comic strips and cartoons were repeated in many of his paintings — huge adults drawn from a child's perspective, tiny figures confronted by a vast expanse of sea and sky, angularities that were reflected in his modified Cubism. He acknowledged the direct link, but he was the exception. Stylistic elements in the graphic work of some — van Dongen, Crane, Bellows and Marsh, for example — are found also in their canvases; but since these artists were painting while drawing for periodicals, their paintings may have influenced their graphic style, and not vice versa. Some of the early representational paintings of Kupka and Villon closely resembled their graphic work in style and content; but when they shifted to more abstract painting, the connection was broken. One could speculate that Vallotton and Forain may have developed into better painters if they had not spent so many years doing graphic work for publication. Except for Crane's, the caricatures of the English painters were a world apart from their solemn canvases. About two-thirds of the artists represented here show no stylistic relationship between their graphic commentaries and their paintings.

This selection is concerned with the nineteenth and twentieth centuries, beginning with Delacroix. However, the caricatures and cartoons of Delacroix and the others presented here did not spring full-blown. An evolutionary process led to the creation of the several forms of graphic satire. Since an historic continuum shaped them, let us take a very brief look.

Satirical depiction of figures and situations is almost as ancient as art itself.[2] In Egyptian papyri there is a touch of parody in the creation of animals playing human roles, and on Greek vases even the gods are lampooned occasionally. The Romans, too, portrayed animals acting out human foibles. For the most part, however, such ancient arts only show that many peoples have had a sense of the ridiculous, a feeling for satire; none of them was caricature in today's sense. They did not portray specific individuals, reveal insight into character or satirize social or political institutions.

A thin vein of satire was mined in the Middle Ages by sculptors who carved church decorations and misericords and by talented monks who made marginal illuminations on manuscripts.[3] But anthropomorphic doodling and scatological scenes did little to enlarge the scope of satire or broaden the approach to caricature. Perhaps only the leveling theme of the Dance of Death, later so hauntingly portrayed in Holbein's woodcuts, was the principal contribution of the Middle Ages to satire beginning to verge on caricature.

With the dissemination of books, broadsheets and prints during the Reformation, crude situation caricatures or political cartoons, which had appeared sporadically, began to be produced in abundance. The Cranachs and Holbein attacked the Pope, pictured him as an offspring of the Devil, a corrupt dispenser of indulgences. In the counterattack, Luther was portrayed as collaborator of the Devil, and the battle was joined with woodcarver's knife and engraver's burin.[4] A new dimension — content — emerged. Artists, great and minor, were veering toward political caricature.

In seventeenth-century Holland, as peace gradually prevailed, broadsheets containing mild social satire became popular,[5] precedents for the flowering of caricature in seventeenth-century England. During the reign of Louis XIV of France, the Protestant exile Cornélis Dusart introduced a new element in the progression toward portrait caricature — emblematic caricature. In a book of 25 caricatures of the Sun King and his entourage,[6] Dusart frequently used symbols to make his points. His hooded, torch-bearing Inquisitor has no face — only the emblem of the Sun — drawn almost 300 years before today's editorial-page cartoon.

An equally significant development was taking place in Italy. Annibale Carracci, followed in this area by his brother Agostino and by Bernini, Guercino, later Tiepolo,[7] invented what developed into "portrait caricature," which seizes upon a facial feature and exaggerates it, leaving the subject's face recognizable but distorted in a way to provide insight into his character. Mannerism probably provided the Carracci brothers and their followers with the stimulus of exaggeration. However, their distortions were mild by comparison with Leonardo's grotesqueries, which he drew as studies in physiognomy or pathology.

> Annibale Carracci is purported to have argued:
>> Is not the caricaturist's task exactly the same as that of the classical artist? Both see the lasting truth beneath the surface of mere outward appearance. Both try to help nature accomplish its plan. The one may strive to realize it in his work, the other to grasp their perfect deformity, and thus reveal the very essence of a personality.[8]

The verb "caricare" means "to overload," which is indeed the word for the kind of savage caricatures spawned by Rowlandson, Gillray and others during the censor-free periods of late-eighteenth-century England. The free-

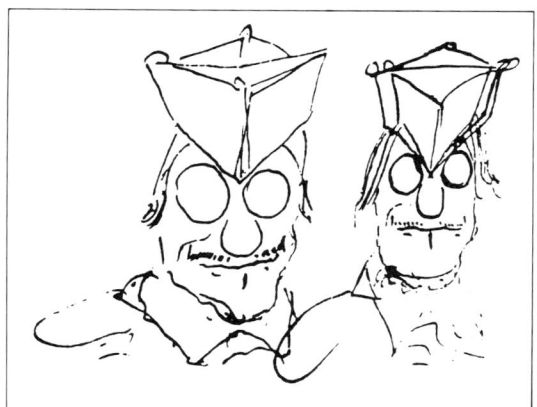

G. L. Bernini *Two Priests Wearing Eyeglasses*. Vatican Library, Rome.

Cornélis Dusart *Le Roy de France*, 1691. Mezzotint. 5⅝ x 4¼. Prints Division, New York Public Library.

G. D. Tiepolo *The Swing*, c. 1791. Pen and brown ink and wash. 10 x 13⅞. Wadsworth Atheneum, Hartford.

wheeling atmosphere provided fertile ground for the blossoming of their bawdy, zestful, hyperbolic caricatures.[9] Wildly exaggerated in both drawing and content, they lacked the relative restraints of the moralistic homilies of Hogarth. He had disdained the facial distortions of caricature but paved the way for political and social caricature with his masterful "The Times" and "Gin Lane."

The nineteenth century witnessed the perfecting of a major component in the galaxy of caricatures — the *portrait charge* — the depiction of a personality which the artist achieves by enlarging the head, exaggerating salient characteristics of the face, and frequently shrinking or tapering the body — sometimes gentle satire, often ridicule. In France, in the periods when censorship was lifted, the *portrait charge* in the talented hands of a Daumier and some of his successors became a merciless instrument for exposing corruption, cupidity, complacence, vanity and frailty. As Ernst Gombrich said of the practitioner of *portrait charge*, "With a few strokes, he may unmask the public hero, belittle his pretentions, and make a laughing stock of him."[10]

By the mid-nineteenth century, the armory of the caricaturist or cartoonist was complete, including the narrative form, as practiced by Hogarth and developed by Töpffer and Wilhelm Busch, which led eventually to the comic strip. Caricatures portrayed people; cartoons and situation caricatures satirized their behavior. Cartoons were political, or social, or simply humorous, or all three. By the mid-nineteenth century, the humorous cartoon had completed the gamut with "he-she" and gag.

The nineteenth century also witnessed fundamental shifts in each nation's use of caricature. In genteel Victorian England, the vitriol of a Gillray was gradually transmuted to sugared lemon juice, and caricature reverted to the mildly humorous style of seventeenth-century Italy. Gillray's savage onslaughts were succeeded by the bland, at times well-drawn, joshing of *Punch* and the only occasionally barbed satire of *Vanity Fair*.[11] While caricature and cartoon took off in France, they were harnessed into respectability in England. "The Parisians say of our Victorian caricaturists that they smile rather than laugh," commented one observer.[12] Outlets were limited. Perhaps it was because, except for the Chartist movement, England's political progression was relatively orderly. There was no Revolution as in France, no violent upheavals to inflame passions and leave a radical aftermath. The Industrial Revolution came early to England. While men, women and children worked into the night before returning to the proliferating hovels, the middle class laughed at *Punch* (or perhaps nodded when *Punch* occasionally reminded its readers that there was real poverty in England), and sublimated their passions in the romance of the Empire. *Punch* satirized middle-class foibles and lower-class weaknesses, but never — well, hardly ever — made its audience wince. Genteel England was titillated by *Vanity Fair*, which never crossed the boundaries of good taste. Only caricatures of foreign rulers had any political substance. Not until the last decades of the century, when the gospel of

Socialism was spread in a number of periodicals, did anti-capitalist cartoons appear. Artists like Ford Madox Brown, Frank Holl, and Luke Fildes painted scenes of labor and poverty but made no caricatures. Most English painters were oriented toward society, not alienated from it. Some of them, as presented here, found an outlet for their satirical impulses in lighthearted, good-humored caricatures of hosts, hostesses, friends and themselves, often drawn after long weekends in the country, or in letters — all very private, rarely for publication. They found in caricatures a release from the uptight restrictions of a corseted English society.

Nineteenth-century France, however, responded enthusiastically to every type of caricature and cartoon. Even Ingres, using the anagrammatic pseudonym of "Regni," made sketches that bordered upon caricature. Especially when censorship was lifted, thousands of political, social and humorous cartoons were published, all eagerly welcomed by the public. There were several reasons for this.

It was a century of political upheavals, with revolutions, war, colonial rivalries, prolonged conflicts between Church and anti-clericals, struggles to extend the electorate and to recapture the fruits of the Revolution, all bringing years of turmoil alternating with periods of relative calm and prosperity. The Industrial Revolution brought inevitable exploitation, unemployment, heightened tensions. Recurrent agricultural crises discharged a flood of unemployed farm laborers into the cities, creating still more dislocations. All these stresses made the stuff of political cartoons for the social-minded caricaturist — when the censor did not clamp down, as he did frequently under the Restoration, later continuously from 1835 to 1868, from '71 to '79, and periodically thereafter. Especially during the last quarter of the century, political caricature and cartoon became less parochial, more concerned with the dangers of war and social and class hostilities.

France had a strong traditional interest in the theory that facial characteristics and gestures reveal character. Near the end of the seventeenth century, Charles Le Brun had written a manual[13] that purported to show painters the expressions and gestures that best express both emotion and character. For more than a century, uninspired painters memorized it. J.C. Lavater, in his immensely popular late-eighteenth-century treatise[14] on the art of interpreting men by their physiognomy, claimed to demonstrate how external appearances reveal character. From 1823 to 1828, Louis-Léopold Boilly made 16 lithographs of grimacing faces, their expressions distorted; a large public studied them. All Paris watched eyebrows, shapes of nose and chin, for clues to character. They carefully observed gestures as keys to behavior, and crowded into the pantomime theatres, where expression and gesture were honed to a fine emblematic art.[15] This preoccupation with movements of face and body provided a ready audience for caricature and a profusion of symbols that could be interpreted instantly.

A technical development — the invention of lithography — also spurred the dissemination of caricature by enabling the artist to draw directly on the stone, simplifying and improving the reproduction of line drawings.

At the right time a genius appeared who lifted caricature to the realm of art. And a vehicle was provided by Charles Philipon, publisher of *La Silhouette*, then of *La Caricature* and *Le Charivari*, journals that reached an audience already visually educated. For 40 years Honoré Daumier fought for such fundamental concepts as freedom, peace and democracy; when censorship tightened, he satirized the comedy of manners being played out on the streets of Paris. "The live and staring corpse, the plump and well-filled corpse, the ridiculous troubles of the home, every little stupidity, every enthusiasm, every despair of the bourgeoisie — it is all there,"[16] wrote Baudelaire on Daumier's social satires. His remarkable insights into the foibles, ambitions, fears and conceits of middle-class Parisians at home and abroad — that is, 20 miles from Paris in the perilous jungles of semi-rural France — are an imperishable record, unmatched in its artistry. Like Baudelaire, Champfleury and Théophile Gautier recognized Daumier's artistic value; all three found it more vigorous than Salon painting.

Except for Daumier, there are almost no painters as caricaturists who contributed to publications in mid-nineteenth-century France (at least no painters regarded now as significant), mainly because they were so Salon-oriented, concerned with mythological, classical and historical themes, landscape and anecdotal genre. Some drew caricatures privately. Only with the gradual acceptance of Impressionism and its focus on everyday reality did painters in considerable numbers turn to cartooning for financial or stylistic reasons. "Rather incline toward caricature than toward prettiness," Pissarro advised his painter-son Lucien, "and study Charles Keene [of *Punch*]."[17]

Daumier's last drawings were made in the early years of the Third Republic. In the following decades he had many notable successors who drew for an extraordinary number and variety of publications, unmatched in any country at any time. From 1870 to 1900 in Paris alone, 139 weeklies and monthlies specializing in caricatures and cartoons were published, some short-lived, some appearing throughout the entire period. (In contrast, only half a dozen reviews devoted to the satire of manners appeared during the July monarchy.) Another 94 were launched between 1900 and 1914. In addition, 96 dailies and weeklies that published caricatures and cartoons but did not feature them appeared between 1870 and 1900.[18] This was an enormous market that hungry artists raced to supply. And hungry most of them were, especially at the turn of the century. From all over France and Europe they poured into Paris. By 1909, the number of painters exhibiting at the Société des Indépendants reached the incredible total of 6,701.[19] Unknowns had little chance of earning a living through painting; inevitably, the journals beckoned to some. Artists such as Kupka, Luce and Vallotton, later van Dongen, Gris, and Marcoussis, maintained themselves — when they got paid — by drawing cartoons for the "*journaux amusants*" or the more politically oriented weeklies. Jacques Villon received 50 francs a drawing from *Le Courrier Français*, but he had to chase after it. He recalls trailing the editor: "His carriage used to come for him every morning at 7:30 and when we wanted to get any money... you had to catch him before 7 o'clock. For night prowlers, it was best not to go to bed."[20]

Woman as a sex object was a staple in dozens of journals. Lightly clad or unclad female figures flitted through their pages. Or they were fully clothed — often beautifully — and usually preoccupied with the interplay of the sexes. Prostitutes and demi-mondaines figured prominently, but only in the radical magazines was prostitution attacked as an institution.

As Joel Isaacson has observed, "For the most part, the illustrators addressed themselves to a male audience, to the would-be man of the world. The cartoonist was a popular artist; to a considerable degree he was the 'painter' of the middle class and for the middle class, of and for that class which, in its extraordinary rise to prominence and at least marginal wealth within the expanded urban setting, provided the occasion for the existence of these images in the first place."[21]

Many of the *journaux amusants* were light, frothy, full of gags, gentle satires and, in some cases, nude girls — Belle Epoque versions of *Playboy* centerfolds, but the idealized figures were sketched, not photographed. Toulouse-Lautrec, Forain, Willette, Aubrey Beardsley and many whose work was not far below theirs brightened the pages of the weeklies. Several artists — Villon and Kupka, later Gris and Marcoussis — courageously gave up their relatively lucrative cartooning to work full time on paintings for which there was little or no audience. Ironically, as Jean Adhémar has pointed out,[22] the journals for which they drew then attacked their paintings.

After the law of July 29, 1881, loosened the tight censorship of the Third Republic (an artist even had to obtain permission of his subject before he could publish a *portrait charge*), there was an outpouring of lightly satirical magazines and eventually more visually oriented political journals unseen in Paris since Louis-Philippe had cracked down on Philipon's publications in 1835. Even *Le Courrier Français*, which specialized in scenes of Montmartre life, published drawings on Boulanger and Dreyfus, as did *L'Illustration*, and *Le Rire* frequently published political satires.

About 1880 photogravure was introduced in France and greatly improved the quality of reproduction. Thousands upon thousands of hasty, routine sketches appeared in the vast number of ephemeral journals, and hundreds of well-conceived, well-drawn caricatures or cartoons came off the presses, some regarded so seriously by the artists that they later turned them into prints.

Paris streets were filled with the inevitable by-products of a nation in the turmoil of a new industrialism without the safety valve of social services. The poor, the homeless, the castoffs were only too visible to young artists, themselves struggling. Many of the more social-minded turned to anarchism as the political expression of their response to the obvious injustices. Requiring little commitment or participation, stressing the fulfillment of the individual, it had a strong appeal to artists and writers. Pissarro, Signac, Angrand, Cross, van Rysselberghe, van Dongen, Kupka — all contributed to Jean Grave's anarchist publication, *Les Temps Nouveaux*. The ever-involved Luce and Steinlen drew for the anarchist *Père Peinard*, the socialist *Le Chambard socialiste*, and just about every journal of the left. As Ernst Gombrich commented, "Humour is not a necessary weapon in the cartoonist's armoury."[23]

The goal of the social-minded artist was to be accepted by *L'Assiette au Beurre*[24] (1901-12), a weekly with 16 pages, 8½" x 10½", at least half in color, and little or no text. Almost 10,000 drawings, most of them full-page, appeared during its 12 years of publication. Often one artist illustrated an entire issue; frequently he could choose his own subject and vent his spleen against monopolies, prostitution, colonialism, capitalism, the Catholic church, the bureaucracy, the military, the prejudiced courts, or especially the crowned heads of Europe. "We were all anarchists without throwing bombs, we had those kinds of ideas,"[25] Kees van Dongen recalled. Not all issues were political; for protective coloration, the editor often devoted satirical issues to innocuous topics — dentists, mothers-in-law, and other international staples from the cartoonist's bottom drawer. No magazine in any country could match the roll call of its contributors, who were later to become famous as painters or graphic artists — Villon, Kupka, van Dongen, Forain, Vallotton, Gris, Marcoussis, Alfred Kubin, Steinlen. Even the poster artist Jules Chéret illustrated an entire frothy issue with his seductive Cherettes. Artists from many countries read it and contributed to it.

With exceptions — such as Pissarro, Signac and Luce — few of these artists retained their youthful radical views. Most trod the familiar path from radical to liberal to conservative or indifferent. As they grew older or more successful or simply wholly involved in painting, they turned inward, away from a distracting world. Many less-successful painters clung to their radicalism and frequently continued their satirical graphic work for publication; some were perhaps trapped or enticed by fairly regular income. Possibly their failure to pursue their painting single-mindedly may have kept them from reaching their artistic peak.

Surprisingly, few *portraits charges* appear here. During the latter part of the century, the French preoccupation with physiognomical significance faded and the satiric possibilities of situation caricature had more appeal to artists. The comedy of manners, the ironies that marked daily existence, sexual byplay, social and political injustice rather than specific individuals involved the caricaturists.

In nineteenth-century Germany, most caricature and cartoon were light and humorous, including the pioneering comic strips of Wilhelm Busch and Adolph Oberlander, imaginative and inoffensive. Germans were amused but not stirred to passion by the artists in the everlasting *Fliegende Blätter*, to which Lyonel Feininger contributed. In 1896, however, political and social satire in Germany, hitherto confined to *ULK*, the newspaper supplement, and a few journals, forced itself on the German consciousness with the debut of *Simplicissimus*, Germany's most influential satirical magazine. With a host of distinguished graphic artists, *"der Simpl"* attacked the same subjects that the French left lampooned — the military, the church, the self-satisfied middle class, the bureaucracy, etc.; but it ran into trouble — more serious trouble than its French counterparts had encountered — when it scoffed at the Kaiser's foreign policy. Two artists were jailed; the publisher fled for several years. After World War I, when it supported the government, *Simplicissimus* gradually declined. Although a number of outstanding graphic artists contributed to it — Kollwitz, Kubin, Steinlen, Willette, Gulbransson, Heine, Thony, among others — the only leading painters in its pages were Grosz and Pascin. The prolific Grosz also appeared in the radical but short-lived *Neue Jugend, Die Röte Erde, Der Querschnitt* and several others of the post-World War I period. Despite its possible contribution to German Expressionism — and Expressionism's influence on Grosz and other caricaturists — caricature for publication did not attract the painters.

As in Germany, painters in America were late in arriving at caricature. Nast and Keppler had rescued American political cartooning from the loutish excesses and inept imitations of Gillray in the early days of the Republic. And caricature, the democratic art, was greeted with chortles in democratic America, especially when its victims were politicians. Although Winslow Homer privately made drawings that were weakly satirical, nineteenth-century American painters were, for the most part, lofty of vision and disdainful of caricature. *Puck* and *Life* seemed to have little interest for them. With the launching of *The Masses*,[26] however, political cartoons suddenly acquired character and imagination. Talented artists — Bellows, Sloan, Davis, and some lesser members of the Ashcan School — made graphic comments on American society. Unpaid and idealistic, most of them were vaguely oriented toward socialism. With some exceptions, their attacks on America's obvious failings were tempered by humor; their satire lacked the savage hatred of Kupka and others. *The Masses* had a bouyancy missing from the French and German counterparts on which it was based — *Le Rire, Simplicissimus, Jugend*. The cartoons tended to be representational, illustrative, closer to Steinlen than to any other French artist.

The kind of cartoon which suddenly flowered in *The Masses* slowly withered in the pages of its successors: *The Liberator* and especially *The New Masses*, where shrill tone and didactic atmosphere marred and weakened the work. Humorous cartoons flourished in *The New Yorker*, but Reginald Marsh was the only significant painter to appear in it.

Abstract Expressionism was so antithetical to caricature or cartoon that during the Vietnam War most painters felt helpless to express their opposition except by contributing abstract prints to fund-raising portfolios. The representational painters rarely advanced beyond the cliché. A number of other painters have employed a cartoon vocabulary for visual expression — among them, H.C. Westermann, Red Grooms, Roy Lichtenstein, and Philip Guston, who told his students to learn cartooning. Some of the slashed faces that loom out of de Kooning's canvases seem to stem from caricature's ancient technique of distortion. With Pop Art, cartoon becomes artifact.

Thus, there is a continuum of satire from Egyptian papyrus to *The New Yorker*, a tradition of caricature and cartoon by painters from Annibale Carracci and Hans Holbein to Gauguin and Picasso.

Of the artists represented and discussed in the following pages, these may be considered "Sunday caricaturists": Pissarro, Manet, Puvis de Chavannes, Picasso, Rossetti, Millais, Burne-Jones, Landseer and Sickert. Eyebrows may be raised at inclusion of the prolific Picasso — but he did not draw his numerous caricatures for publication.

Many caricaturists of the nineteenth and early twentieth centuries who achieved reputations as painters in their time are not included here because today their painting seems parochial or limited. The paintings of the most ferocious and funniest French caricaturists, Jean Veber and Charles Léandre (Veber's cartoon of Edward VII as Britannia's *derrière* is the outstanding caricature of the period), were well received — two of Léandre's portraits still hang in the Petit Palais. Hermann-Paul was exhibited by Durand-Ruel, Vollard and Bernheim Jeune. Doré, a precocious caricaturist, was acclaimed as a painter in London and Paris. Félix Régamey taught painting at the Ecole des Arts Decoratifs. T.A. Steinlen was one of the greatest political cartoonists; today his paintings seem to be an extension of his graphic work. The landscapist Fernand Gottlob, who contributed frequently to *L'Assiette au Beurre, Sourire, La Vie en Rose* and others, had a large retrospective of his paintings in Paris in 1938; Albert Guillaume, pupil of Gérôme, contributed to the light magazines and was highly regarded as a painter in his day. Today their reputations as painters have faded. Lear was the master of caricature, but his landscapes seem pallid today. Among the American cartoonists who were also painters, George Luks now seems to us a lesser member of the Ashcan School, Boardman Robinson's paintings too closely resemble illustrations, and William Gropper now appears to have played one note.

A number of French nineteenth-century "official" Salon painters caricatured themselves or their friends[27] — Decamps, Couture and Regnault, among others — and Charles Jacque and Horace Vernet published caricatures in their early years, Jacque appearing in *Le Charivari*; but their paintings lack the appeal today that they had a century ago.

Several painters are not represented in the text because their satirical work was so infrequent — artists like Henri-Edmond Cross, de Chirico, Masson, Miró, Rousseau, Dunoyer de Segonzac. Cross's work appeared only occasionally in *Les Temps Nouveaux*. De Chirico's amusing sketch, shown here, portrays Picasso and friends at table, under Rousseau's self-portrait. Masson and Miró drew upon carica-

William Hogarth *Satire on Perspective*, 1754. Engraving. 8¼ x 6¾. British Museum, London.

Henri Rousseau *War*, **L'Imagier**, 1895. Transfer lithograph. 8¾ x 13. Museum of Modern Art, New York.

ture to express their hatred of Franco during the Spanish Civil War. Rousseau's single effort, published in *L'Imagier*, was one of the greatest portrayals of war as idiot's delight. Barlach drew for *Simplicissimus*, but he was primarily a sculptor. Whistler is not here because attribution of some of his caricatures is being questioned. Ensor, Rouault, Dix and Beckmann are not included because they were primarily printmakers and rarely, if ever, worked for the journals. Other German painters, such as Corinth, Marc, Heckel and Kirchner, frequently had their work published in periodicals, but it was more decorative or illustrative than caricatural. When *Der Bildermann*, a beautiful magazine with a pacifist theme, was published briefly in 1916, Heckel could draw only an allegorical Belgian landscape as a mild rebuke for the German invasion, Kirchner was more elusive than allusive, and Kokoschka resorted to scenes from the life of Christ. Only the lesser Slevogt was direct, with a series of 10 anti-war cartoons. Klee's ironic fantasies and allegories defy category. Living cartoonists or caricaturists who are painters as well are not included here; time will best tell how they will be remembered.

And where are the women painters as caricaturists? Not here. Of 167 caricaturists listed in Lethève's *La Caricature et La Presse sous la IIIe République*,[28] only one is a woman (there may have been a few more, hiding behind genderless pseudonyms). Cassatt, Morisot, Gonzales, Bracquemond, for example, seem to have had no interest in caricature, nor economic need to work in it. Among the struggling artists of *fin-de-siècle* France, there were doubtless some women who were the equals of many of the cartoonists in the lighter journals and who may have shared the political outlook of the artists in the more radical publications. But publishing was a man's world. Women had no vote, made little progress in the professions, and encountered all sorts of barriers, social, economic and political. When they tried to get equal rights, even Daumier had satirized them, in the "Bluestocking" series.

In England, the few nineteenth-century women artists were not caricaturists. In Germany, the great graphic artist, Käthe Kollwitz, who contributed to *Simplicissimus*, was not a painter, while the work of Paula Modersohn-Becker, which appeared in several German periodicals, was illustrative rather than satirical. In the United States, talented women caricaturists appeared in *The New Yorker*, but they were not painters or, like Peggy Bacon's, their painting was mostly an extension of their satirical work.

If it seems paradoxical that Daumier and Goya are not included here, it is because they have been so widely exhibited, dissected and published that it would be redundant to present them again. Besides, to do them adequate justice would require a separate book and exhibition.

This collection is selective, not definitive; exhibition space limitations prevent it from being more encyclopedic. The painters here are presented chronologically by country, from Delacroix, the first to be born, to Picasso, the last to die. Some of these artists are ambiguous in their nationality.

Pascin was born in Bulgaria, drew most of his cartoons for German publications, became an American citizen, but ended up Parisian to the core. Grosz and Feininger held U.S. citizenship, but their major caricatural work was drawn for publication in Germany. Tissot was born in France and fought in the Commune, but his caricatures are English in content and style.

Today, caricature and cartoon have moved from pen and paper to brush and canvas. Distinctions between them have long been broken down. The distortions, the emblematic qualities, the abstractions of caricature are integrated into so much of contemporary painting that its uniqueness as an art form is diminishing. As Steinberg and others have shown, caricature can take new forms. And artists to come will doubtless create as yet unimagined conceptions. The only certainty is that future caricaturists will never run out of material.

Notes to "Painters as Caricaturists and Cartoonists"

When only author cited, see Bibliography for title and date and place of publication.

1. Dora Villier, *Jacques Villon*, Paris, n.d., p. 116.
2. For history of Egyptian, Greek and Roman satirical art, see Champfleury (Jules Fleury), *Histoire de la Caricature Antique*, 3rd ed., Paris, 1867; Parton, pp. 15–39; Wright, pp. 1–39.
3. See Dorothy and Henry Kraus, *The Hidden World of Misericords*, New York, 1975; Champfleury, *Histoire de la Caricature au Moyen Age*, Paris, 1871; Parton, pp. 40–63; Wright, pp. 40–213; Lynch, pp. 14–25; Maeterlinck, pp. 20–68.
4. Champfleury, *Histoire de la Caricature sous la Réforme et la Ligue — Louis XIII à Louis XVI*, Paris, 1880; Parton, pp. 64–89; Wright, pp. 244–263; Lynch, pp. 32–42; A. Blum, *L'Estampe Satirique en France pendant les Guerres de la Réligion*, Paris, 1917; A. Hyatt Mayor, "Renaissance Pamphleteers — Savonarola and Luther," *Metropolitan Museum of Art Bulletin*, Oct., 1947, pp. 66–72; H. Grisar and F. Heege, *Luthers Kampfbilder*, 3 vols., Freiburg, 1921–1923; Kunzle, pp. 28–39.
5. C. A. Veth, *Geschiedenis van de Netherlandsche Caricatuur*, Leyden, 1921; C. A. Veth, *De Politicke Prent in Netherland*, Leyden, 1920.
6. Cornélis Dusart, *Les Héros de la Ligue ou La Procession Monacle Conduitte par Louis XIV pour la Conversion de Protestants de Son Royaume*, Paris, 1691.
7. Jean-François Revel, "L'Invention de la Caricature," *l'Oeil*, no. 9, Jan., 1964, pp. 12–21; D. Mahon, *Studies in Seicento Art and Theory*, London, 1947; Gombrich and Kris.
8. Quoted in Feaver, p. 21.
9. The literature of caricature in eighteenth-century England is extensive. See especially both books by George; Klingender; Hill; Parton.
10. Gombrich and Kris, p. 13.
11. For *Vanity Fair*, see especially Matthews and Mellini; also Savory et al.
12. Ashbee, p. 113.
13. Charles Le Brun, *Conférence sur l'expression generale et particulière*, Amsterdam 1698.
14. J. C. Lavater, *Physiognomische Fragmente zur Beförderung der Menschenkuntniss und Menschenliebe*, Leipzig, 1775–1778. English ed., tr. by T. Holcroft, *Essay on Physiognomy, for the Promotion of the Knowledge and the Love of Mankind*, 3 vols., London, 1789.
15. For a thorough and insightful discussion of the influence of Le Brun and Lavater and the relationship of mime to caricature, see Wechsler, chs. 1 and 2.
16. Charles Baudelaire, *The Mirror of Art*, London, 1955, p. 166.
17. John Rewald, ed., *Camille Pissarro: Letters to His Son Lucien*, 3rd ed., Mamaroneck, N.Y., 1972, letter of July 5, 1883, p. 37.
18. Lethève, pp. 241–254. See also Philippe Roberts-Jones, "La Presse satirique illustrée entre 1860 et 1890," *Etudes de Presse*, VIII, no. 14, 1956, pp. 13–14 and his *De Daumier à Lautrec*, Paris 1960; Roger Bellet, *Presse et journalisme sous le deuxième Empire*, Paris, 1967.
19. Cited in Louis Chaumeil, *Van Dongen — L'Homme et l'Artiste*, Geneva, 1967. p. 65.
20. A. Warnod, *Ceux de la Butte*, Paris, 1947, p. 255.
21. Joel Isaacson, "Impressionism and Journalistic Illustration," *Arts*, June, 1982, v. 96, no. 10, p. 96.
22. Jean Adhémar, "Les journeaux amusants et les premiers peintres cubistes," *l'Oeil*, IV, April 15, 1955, pp. 40–43.
23. E. H. Gombrich, "The Cartoonist's Armoury," rep. in his *Meditations on a Hobby Horse*, London, 1963, p. 131.
24. For history and contents of *L'Assiette au Beurre*, see Dixmier; Lambert; Ralph E. Shikes, "Five Artists in the Service of Politics in the Pages of *L'Assiette au Beurre*," ch. in *Art in the Service of Politics*, ed. by Henry A. Millon and Linda Nochlin, Cambridge, Mass., 1978, pp. 162–181.
25. "Bums, Madmen, Masters," *Life*, Feb. 8, 1960, p. 92.
26. For history and contents of *The Masses*, see Fitzgerald: Goldwater; O'Neill. Also Max Eastman, *Love and Revolution: My Journey through an Epoch*, New York, 1964.
27. Aimée Brown Price, "Official Artists and Not-so-Official Art; Covert Caricaturists in Nineteenth-Century France," *Art Journal*, Winter, 1983.
28. Lethève, pp. 255–260.

Giorgio de Chirico *Picasso at Table with Friends*, 1915. Pen and ink. 12¾ x 9¼. Private col.

André Masson *Le Tercio a Sevilla*, 1936. Pen and ink. 18 x 14½. Galerie Louise Leiris, Paris.

In *Le Miroir* he mocked doctors, censors, self-proclaimed actors and artists, returned emigrés, grand opera, and writers for the monarchist and Catholic press. "La Consultation" is a spoof of doctors who chatter and split hairs while their patient dies. In "Le Déménagement," which appeared in *Le Miroir* on February 11, 1822, he celebrates the lifting of censorship. Censor "Sugar Bread" ("Pain" was the name of the chief censor) and his motley crew depart and their censors' scissors fly away, to the consternation of the clerks.

Baudelaire remarked that Delacroix was "passionately in love with passion"; however, except for his consistent devotion to liberty — from his early attack on censorship through his paintings on the Greek revolution to his "Liberty Leading the People" — his passion did not extend to political affairs. Although he was always aware of his revolutionary heritage, he was convinced that nothing changes. He disdained the nouveaux aristocrats of Louis Napoleon's entourage, but he also feared the masses. It is tempting to say that the exuberant movement of Rowlandson's figures carried over into Delacroix's cartoons and thence to the dynamics of his canvases, but the young Delacroix was never really at home in political cartooning. There is a cramped and tight draftsmanship in most of his satirical drawings, and stylistically, the only connection with his painting is the element of exaggeration.

OPPOSITE
Troupes Anglaises, 1816. Lithograph. 8 x 6½. D. 6. Bibliothèque Nationale, Paris.

Le déménagement de la censure, **Le Miroir**, Feb. 11, 1822. Lithograph. 12¼ x 7½. D. 35. Bibliothèque Nationale, Paris.

PUVIS DE CHAVANNES CARICATURISTE

Vous avez bien lu : ces joyeuses caricatures, ce juge à face large qui a l'air de sortir de la troupe de Guignol. Ce paysan couvert jusqu'aux épaules de son chapeau de castor.

Ce membre de l'Institut à l'œil atone, au large ruban sur le revers de l'habit. Ce braconnier prêt à épauler. Cet agent à mine rébarbative. Ces caricatures d'extase enfin, tout cela est bien signé Puvis de Chavannes.

C'est d'un numéro remarquable consacré par la *Plume* à l'œuvre du maître, que nous extrayons ces charges, grâce à l'obligeance de l'actif et artiste directeur, M. Léon Deschamps.

Ne vous étonnez point, bonnes gens, que le grand poète du *Bois sacré* se soit adonné à ces amusements. Rappelez-vous que Victor Hugo fut aussi un caricaturiste désopilant, énorme, et voyez là, une fois de plus, la preuve que les grands rêveurs, les chantres de la pure tendresse, sont aussi, à l'occasion, les plus fins railleurs.

Pierre Cécile Puvis de Chavannes 1824–1898

REJECTED BY THE SALON FOR years, Puvis de Chavannes finally gained such acceptance that he was frequently appointed to the Salon juries. There, his judgments brushed aside, the bored muralist amused himself by sketching caricatures while his more pompous colleagues argued.

His genre paintings now seem sentimental and the allegories of his highly decorative murals sententious; but his innovations and the "primitive" aspect of his work won the admiration of Pissarro and other Impressionists and Neo-Impressionists. According to Sir William Rothenstein, the only picture on Toulouse-Lautrec's studio wall was a photograph of Puvis's "The Sacred Grove."

He drew upon classical, allegorical and religious themes for his murals, motifs of war and peace, of the seasons, and in "Doux Pays," he envisaged an idyllic world of peace and contentment. Like Piero della Francesca, he flattened forms, simplified them and arranged them in decorative patterns effectively enough to exercise considerable influence upon Seurat and Gauguin. "The Sacred Grove" has a direct iconographic kinship to Gauguin's "Whence Come We? Where Are We? Whither Go We?"

His caricatures, some drawn in the studio at the end of a long day, vary from ironic, Daumier-like quick pen strokes to the broad crayon fantasies of a Töpfer. His view of the *comédie humaine* was far from generous. "Beef Butcher" is a macabre, anthropomorphic vision of a world in which slabs of human torsos are suspended from meat hooks while the beef-butcher proudly presides over his gruesome shop. Animals have played human roles in caricature for several thousand years but never to such startling effect. His sketch of family life is equally unflattering and disturbing. In other harsh, Bosch-like fantasies, drawn

OPPOSITE
Group of Sketches, **Le Rire**, Feb. 16, 1895. Col. Mr. and Mrs. Herbert D. Schimmel.
BELOW
Monsignor and his Valet. Pen and ink. Rep. from **Les Caricatures de Puvis de Chavannes**. Bibliothèque Nationale, Paris.

TOP
Beef Butcher. Gouache and crayon. **Ibid.**
BELOW
Un Tour de Valse. Pen and ink. **Ibid.**
OPPOSITE TOP
Family Life. Gouache and crayon. **Ibid.**
OPPOSITE RIGHT
Three Priests. Pen and ink. **Ibid.**

like these, with blunt, emphatic strokes, there is an implication of terror, of a world gone mad.

This painter of religious scenes surprisingly reveals a strong anti-clerical bias in his "Monseigneur et le Valet" and in his malevolent pen portraits of three sanctimonious priests. He was a convivial man who enjoyed galas, but his satirical eye was ever-observant as he sketched the byplay of the sexes, here represented by "Un Tour de Valse."

He could be a deft (and gentle) social commentator, as in the page of satirical portraits — reprinted in *Le Rire* from *La Plume*: a dull member of the Institute so proud of the large ribbon in his lapel, a stern policeman, a snobbish woman, a peasant overwhelmed by his beaver hat. His swift lines get to the core of the personalities. Although he made allegorical drawings for *Cocorico* and other magazines, his satirical work, widely known among his friends, was not originally drawn for publication.

23

Camille Pissarro 1830–1903

Capital, 1889. Pen and brown ink. 12³⁄₁₆ x 9⁷⁄₁₆. Private col., Geneva.

IN THE 1880'S AND FOR SEVERAL decades thereafter, anarchism was the dominant philosophy among French artists, poets and intellectuals who saw the need for change in a society full of inequities. It influenced many of the Neo-Impressionists and, later, the Fauves and Cubists. Spurned by the art establishment and by bourgeois society, avant-garde artists identified with society's economic rejects and were attracted by anarchism's denial of authority and exaltation of the individual.

Of the painters drawn to anarchism, Camille Pissarro was one of its earliest and most devoted adherents, the quintessential intellectual artist, dedicated reader of the works of Proudhon, Reclus and Kropotkin and of the anarchist journals — *La Révolte*, *Père Peinard* and, later, *Les Temps Nouveaux*. Though fierce in his denunciations of a corrupt and oppressive society, he was a somewhat naive follower of anarchism rather than an activist.

Pissarro also had a strong interest in caricature, which he felt had its role in art. He admired the work of Charles Keene, the *Punch* artist, and subscribed to the magazine. Even more did he appreciate Daumier's caricatures in *Charivari*: "You feel in his drawings the sweep of a great artist," he wrote his son Lucien after purchasing Champfleury's *Histoire de la Caricature*.

Pissarro contributed drawings to Jean Grave's *Les Temps Nouveaux*. Although they reflect a sympathy with hard-working peasant women and with homeless wanderers, none is directly agitational. When the editor of *La Plume* asked him for an "anarchist" drawing, Pissarro sent a sketch of stevedores at work and wrote his friend Octave Mirbeau, "Fortunately, I had done this motif during my stay [in Rouen], otherwise I would have been forced to send him a tree trunk, which wouldn't have done the job. I wonder what a man of letters means by 'anarchist'? Something alien it seems to me. Is there an anarchist art? . . . decidedly they don't understand. All art is anarchist! When it is beautiful and good!"

This somewhat amorphous philosophy was reflected in his painting only by his tendency to idealize agricultural life, to portray farming in a healthy rural setting, his idea of anarchism in action.

An occasion arose for Pissarro to combine his interests in anarchism and in caricature when he carried out Kropotkin's exhortation to "show the people the ugliness of contemporary life and make us teach with the finger the cause of this ugliness." In 1889, when he was suffering from the repudiation of his Neo-Impressionist paintings, he made, for his English nieces, a series of acerbic pen-and-ink caricatures which expressed his bitter contempt for French society and his compassion for its victims. He called them "Turpitudes Sociales," later published as a book. Savage and ironical, sentimental and tough, they represent what he called the shameful vices of bourgeois society, except for prostitution, which he felt was too offensive a subject for the delicate sensibilities of his nieces. Eight are captioned by quotations from the anarchist paper *La Révolte*.

The drawings range in mood from satire to blunt preachment, in style from caricature to straightforward graphic representation. Some draw upon Daumier, Hogarth and Cruikshank. Pissarro attacks bankers, speculators, high clergy. He parades life's cruelties — a struggling musician, a failed artist, a homeless child sentenced as a vagabond. In the final episode, workers are fighting on the barricades against government troops.

The opening caricature, appropriately enough, is "Capital," symbol, as he quotes *La Révolte*, "of the war of the dispossessed against the dispossessors, of the lean against the fat, the poor against the rich, life against death." "Capital" represents the "divinity of the day... vulgar and ugly." The well-fed banker hugging "Capital" to his breast lacks the overwhelming power of Kupka's "Mr. Rich" (page 53), but Pissarro is inspired in his massing of emaciated figures, howling, supplicating, threatening, crowding far off to the Seine and the Eiffel Tower, the latter the despised symbol of bourgeois taste. "The poor are many," he is saying.

Pissarro's title for a factory scene is "The Prison," a horror story of exhausted workers and their "proud and conscienceless" patron, "with a slight resemblance to Louis-Philippe," he wrote his nieces. His accompanying quotation from *La Révolte* was classic anarchist dogma. "The poor... are chained to perpetual poverty, kept in ignorance, baseness, misery." It is a night scene, as many in the series are, the darkness enhancing the tensions.

Pissarro eventually became successful, but he never abandoned his belief in anarchism.

The Prison, 1889. Pen and brown ink. 12³⁄₁₆ x 9⁷⁄₁₆. Private col., Geneva.

Edouard Manet 1832–1883

MANET'S TALENT FOR CARICAture made an early bow. At 17, resistant to pursuing his father's career as a magistrate, he compromised with his family and enrolled in the Navy. On a long voyage to Brazil, the commander was so impressed by Manet's sketches of his shipmates that he asked the young sailor to teach drawing. "All the officers and professors have asked me for their caricatures," the proud Manet wrote his mother. Only one of these shipboard sketches has survived; although it has little caricatural quality, his precocious talent as a draftsman is obvious.

Most of Manet's satirical bent was expressed verbally, at the Café Guerbois and in drawing-room ripostes; but caricatural sketches appear occasionally among his drawings, and his graphic oeuvre includes two lithographic caricatures. The *portrait charge* of Ol(l)ivier was reproduced in the weekly *Le Diogène* to illustrate a biography of the French politician, a well-meaning but weak republican liberal who eventually entered Napoleon III's government and led France into the disastrous war of 1870. Manet, who had met Ollivier in Italy, presents him as a calm, thoughtful man, hands crossed, reflective — hence the perfect subject for a *portrait charge*, with its emphasis on the head. But there is a prophetic hint of weakness and self-importance, too, in the face. Clearly this was not a man of action, this "Diogenes."

Of Manet's occasional satirical sketches, most interesting is his portrait of a *diseuse* from the Brasserie de Reichshoffen, "La Belle Polonaise," with its expressive line, the profile of the face and neck forming a sidewise "v." Manet achieves his caricature by simplifying the portrait of the singer and the faces of the orchestra. A less exaggerated profile of the singer appears in the background of his painting "Café-Concert."

He was instinctively a caricaturist, with a sardonically humorous outlook. It is unfortunate that more of his satirical sketches have not survived.

OPPOSITE
Emile Olivier, **Le Diogène**, 1860. Lithograph. 14½ x 9½. Guérin 67. Bibliothèque Nationale, Paris.

LEFT
La Belle Polonaise. Transfer lithograph. 11¼ x 11. Guérin 83. Bibliothèque Nationale, Paris.

LAFERRIÈRE

Claude Monet 1840–1926

As a bored teen-ager at the college of Le Havre, Monet passed the time by drawing caricatures of his teachers and companions. "I garlanded the margins of my notebooks... in the most irreverent way, distorting as much as possible the faces or profiles of my teachers," he recalled. Although only 17, his reputation as a caricaturist spread throughout Le Havre as his friends, to whom he gave his sketches, proudly showed them around. Soon every dignitary in Le Havre felt that he had to have his portrait sketched, no matter how irreverently, by young "Oscar" Monet, as he was known then.

The enterprising young artist, his mother dead in January of 1852, at odds with his father, boldly launched himself. He charged 10 francs, then 20, for a caricature. Orders from local notables poured in after a local framer began to exhibit the drawings every Sunday in the window of his shop. "I used to burst with pride," Monet recalled. To perfect his technique, he copied the caricatures of Nadar, Carjat and Hadol.

The marine-landscape painter Eugène Boudin, impressed by the strength of the drawings, convinced Monet to study painting with him and opened the young man's eyes to nature. In 1858, at 18, Monet exhibited his first landscape. His caricatures not only led indirectly to his career as a landscapist, but the 2,000 francs he earned from them, plus a small subsidy from his father, enabled him to leave for Paris in 1859 to further his training as a painter. In that same year he unsuccessfully

OPPOSITE
Laferrière, **Le Diogène**, March 24, 1860. Bibliothèque Nationale, Paris.
BELOW
Cinq Personnages, c. 1858. Pencil and gouache. 13⅝ x 18⅞. Photo Studio Lourmel 77. Musée Marmottan, Paris.

LEFT
Jules Didier, c. 1859. Charcoal. 23⅝ x 17½.
Art Institute of Chicago.

RIGHT
Rufus Croutinelli, c. 1859. Charcoal. 5½ x 3⅜.
Art Institute of Chicago.

applied to the Municipal Council of Le Havre for a grant of 1,200 francs. Among his rivals for the scholarship was a painter, Henri Cassinelli, who appears in Monet's caricature as "Rufus Croutinelli." Since "croute" is slang for a dead painter, Monet relied on the pun as well as the *portrait charge* to disparage his competitor. His line is precise, the strokes are confident, and the personality of his target emerges strongly even though his style is not original. He does not exaggerate features as much as his contemporaries did; some of his portraits are closer to straight representation than to *portraits charges*. Only rarely did he employ, as in "Cinque Personnages," the physiognomic exaggerations used by the professionals who drew for the newspapers and whom he occasionally copied.

He lets all restraints go in his caricature of Jules Didier, who had won a Prix de Rome in 1857. A perhaps jealous 17-year-old Monet presents him as the head of a butterfly, his bridle held by a female centaur — a prisoner of his award.

For a year or two in Paris Monet continued to draw caricatures, some at the Brasserie des Martyrs, apparently hoping to sell them to newspapers and thus gain steady income. Only one published caricature has been found, however — that of the actor Laferrière, in *Le Diogène* of 24 March, 1860. Possibly he had too much competition; or he may have decided to concentrate on his painting. And Paris was not Le Havre; he did not know the celebrities. In any case, although he did not return to caricature, the acute observation and rapid execution manifested in his caricatures served him well as an Impressionist.

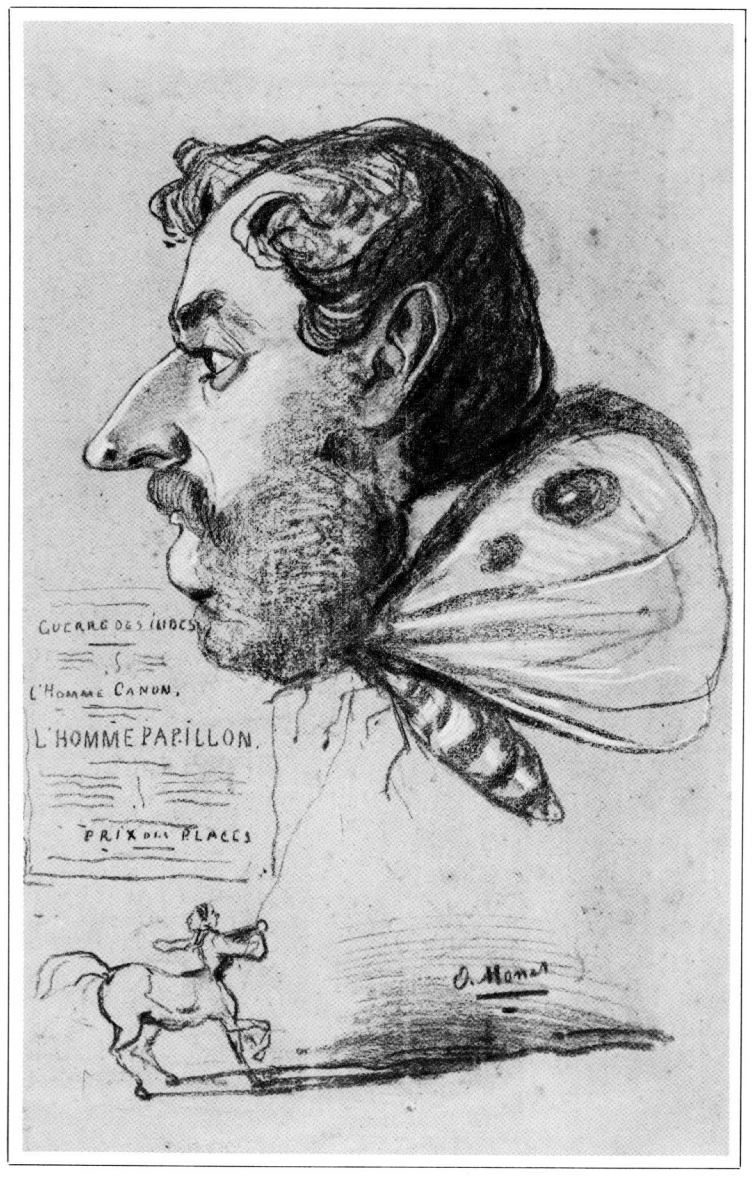

Paul Gauguin 1848–1903

WHEN GAUGUIN WORKED alongside Pissarro in the Seventies, did he absorb his master's love of caricature? Quite possibly, or perhaps this sardonic man was instinctively a caricaturist.

Gauguin displayed a feeling for symbolism close to caricature in the late Eighties and early Nineties. In his self-portrait of 1889 in the National Gallery, Washington, he caricatured himself as a fallen saint with symbols of halo, snake and apples, a Satanic expression on his arrogant face. Two years later, he drew "Soyez Symboliste" for *La Plume*, with Jean Moréas, the Symbolist poet and author of the Symbolist manifesto, portrayed as enigmatic, peering fiercely into the unknown, a prophet glimpsing the future, surrounded by the elusive symbols of peacock and seraph.

But these were only peripherally caricatural. Gauguin's satirical talent burst into full bloom only in the nourishing climate of the tropics. His last years in Tahiti were demoralizing. Penniless, he applied for a position as treasurer of the Agricultural Bank. Scornfully rejected by Governor Gallet, humiliated, he accepted a job as draftsman in Public Works at six francs a day, losing his status among the class-conscious civil servants. Forced to move nearer his job, his anger at the administration exploded when the procurator refused even to investigate petty thievery in and around his empty house.

His resentment poured forth in a letter to *Les Guêpes (The Wasps)*, a new local paper, in June, 1899. "That's how I became a journalist, a polemicist, if you prefer," he commented. In July he attacked Governor Gallet for neglecting the interests of the French settlers and he began to contribute regularly, becoming a hero of the local French community, which despised the civil administrators sent by Paris. To capitalize on his new-found talent, he also started his own hand-written, mimeographed newspaper, *Le Sourire*, on August 21, 1899, and was soon deeply involved in the internecine, and meaningless, warfare between the so-called "Catholic" and "Protestant" parties. Since *Les Guêpes* was the organ of the Catholic party, Gauguin (incredibly — only three years before, he had written an anti-Catholic diatribe) wrote articles attacking the Protestant missionaries as well as the administration. In January, 1900, he accepted the editorship of *Les Guêpes* and four months later

TOP
Soyez Symboliste, **La Plume**, Jan. 1, 1891. Col. Mr. and Mrs. Herbert D. Schimmel. (Original: Brush and pen and ink. 13¾ x 16½.)

BOTTOM
Magot de la Guadeloupe, **Les Guêpes**, c.1900. New York Public Library.

dropped *Le Sourire*, from which he had never made more than 50 francs a month. Altogether, his journalistic career lasted two years, from June 12, 1899, to July 18, 1901, a period during which he did not paint.

Gauguin not only wrote numerous signed and unsigned articles, some signed "Tit-Oil," but also drew a number of cartoons for both publications. The hated Governor Gallet became "Gaspard" in cartoons and articles. In this delightful woodcut for a cover of *Le Sourire*, Gallet is dreaming of a dynasty, with crown floating above the bedstead, the cartoon drawn with Gauguin's inelegant but powerful and firm draftsmanship.

Rankling at an earlier rejection by former Governor Lacascade for a post as magistrate, Gauguin avenged himself by drawing Lacascade barefoot, implying that he was black, with his aide carrying a baby labelled "Magot," which means both "treasure" and "baboon." He was playing on the rumor that Lacascade had amassed a fortune through bribery. He pursued the same theme in "Gaspard et son petit Page." A crowned Gallet is a bear about to gorge himself on the "honey" of Tahiti, the monkey being Secretary-General Rey.

His articles were repetitive, boring, paid hackwork; his cartoons, amusing and effective. Both were yellow journalism, wildly exaggerated, vengeful distortions. Gauguin has often been depicted as crusading on behalf of the oppressed natives; as Bengt Danielsson has made clear, he was simply representing the reactionary interests of the settlers. At one meeting of the Catholic party, he orated his version of the "yellow peril" by denouncing the influx of Chinese (who were competing with the French merchants). When Vollard offered to send him a steady remittance, he dropped journalism to return to painting and soon left for the Marquesas in search of a purer and more primitive native population.

While he was editing *Les Guêpes*, Gauguin liked to give dinner parties for his neighbors and a few friends, with formal "menus," which he often illustrated, as in this cartoon of the local police chief.

Gauguin was grinding a personal and financial axe in his attacks on the government, but possibly there was a deeper, subconscious instinct at work, a residue of the anarchism of his grandmother Flora Tristran, of Pissarro, of some of his Symbolist friends. He was contradictory: hostile to accepted conventions, but more frequently than not a supporter of the French government in its colonialism. "He is always on the side of the bastards," Pissarro decried — but at times he was a rebel with a dream. Shortly before he died in the Marquesas, he advocated abolition of bureaucracy and monopoly and called for a rule of "reason, humanity, fraternity and charity." Alas, only rarely had he himself lived by any of these lofty principles.

Gaspard et son Petit Page, **Les Guêpes**, 1900. 9½ x 7¼. New York Public Library.

Menu, c. 1901. Rep. from **Onze Menus de Paul Gauguin**. 7½ x 6⅛. New York Public Library.

Le Sourire, 1899–1900. Metropolitan Museum of Art. (Original: Woodcut. 10½ x 6½. Guérin 83.)

Distraction

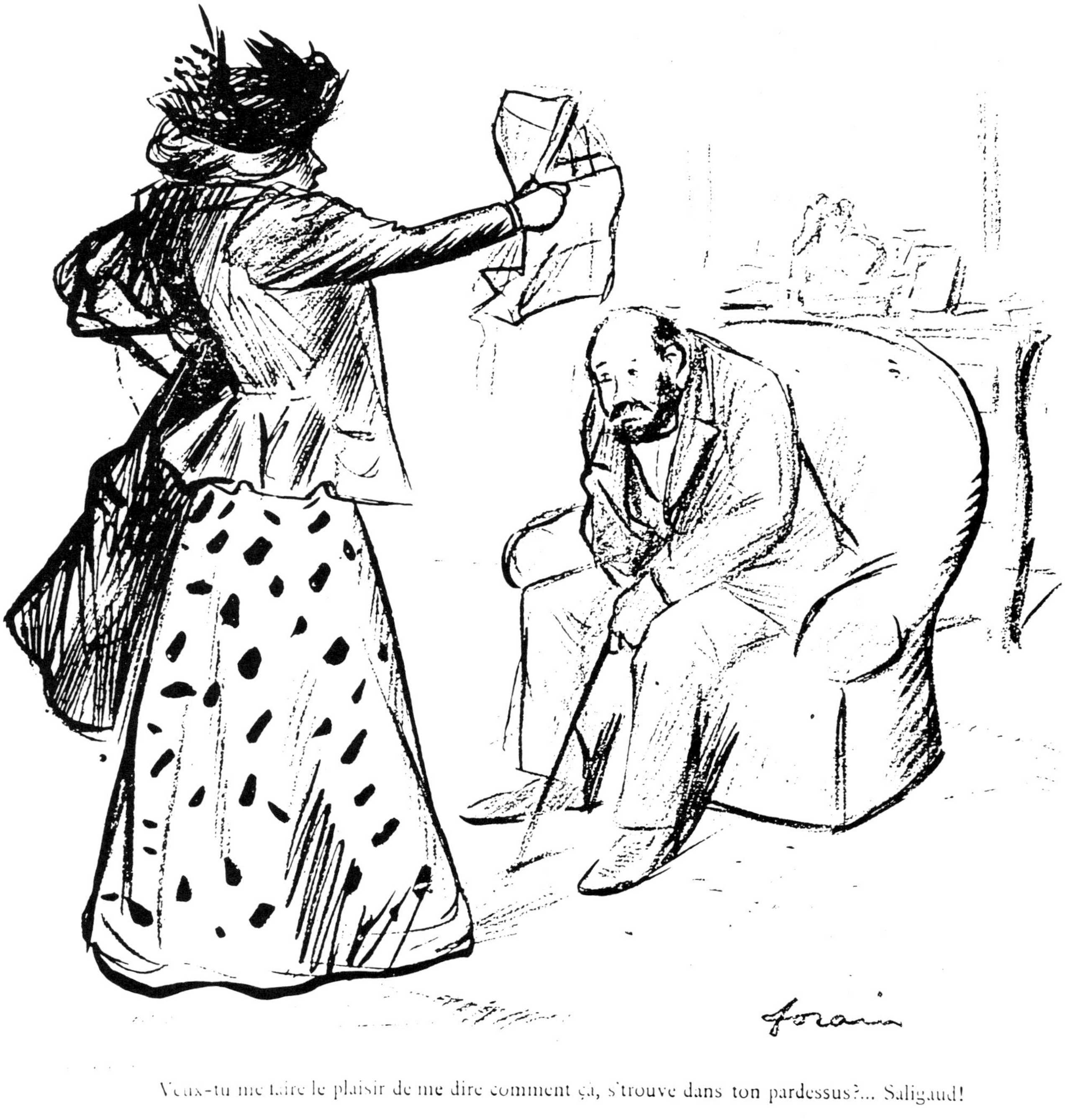

Veux-tu me faire le plaisir de me dire comment ça, s'trouve dans ton pardessus?... Saligaud!

Jean-Louis Forain 1852–1931

TOUT PARIS AWAITED FORAIN'S cartoons in *Le Courrier Français* and *Le Figaro*, as well as in *Gil Blas*, *L'Echo de Paris* and others. For a time in the Nineties he drew a hundred cartoons a year for *Le Courrier Français* and his work appeared in *Le Figaro* for more than 30 years. Degas bought his drawings and prints and displayed them in his studio, Cézanne hung his cartoons on his studio walls, Lautrec admired them, Gauguin took three of Forain's drawings with him when he left France for Denmark.

His drawings of Parisian life in a variety of magazines presented a collective portrait of money-grubbers — whether businessmen, politicians, or professionals, and even mothers willing to sell their daughters — of middle-aged lechers with young mistresses, of justifiably jealous wives, of a sex-ridden milieu. Edmond de Goncourt noted that "Ce Forain a une langue toute Parisienne." It was a sardonic portrait, contemptuous and cynical. He rarely evoked laughter, as Daumier did, although stylistically he drew upon Daumier until he evolved his own touch.

That touch became firm and accurate, his stroke decisive and economical, his figures expressive. Significant background was indicated by a few telling strokes. He became a master draftsman, but because of his vast output, his lines were sometimes hasty, his faces without individuality, his figures wooden, and when he ignored the technical demands of the printing press, his contrasts became attenuated.

He assailed the injustices of society, sympathized with its victims, satirized the materialism of the middle class, yet he strove for financial success (and achieved it) and aspired (successfully) to gain the middle class he supposedly despised. Anarchist editor Jean Grave observed acutely of Forain, "what a bourgeois soul he often hides beneath his hatred." He edited and illustrated, with

OPPOSITE
Distraction, **Le Courrier Français**, May 17, 1896.
Col. Mr. and Mrs. Herbert D. Schimmel.

BOTTOM LEFT
L'Amour à Paris, **Le Fifre**, March 9, 1889.
Col. Mr. and Mrs. Herbert D. Schimmel.

BOTTOM RIGHT
A l'Opéra, **Le Courrier Français**, Nov. 13, 1887.
Col. Mr. and Mrs. Herbert D. Schimmel.

Caran d'Ache, *Psst!*, a virulent anti-Semitic magazine during the Dreyfus affair; yet a few years later he engraved a moving and sensitive series on society's victims in the courtroom. He became an extreme nationalist — he enlisted at 62 in World War I — and deeply religious.

In "Distraction," the outraged wife confronts her husband with another woman's corset she found in his overcoat. His aim is sure, his line strong. You feel her indignation and his guilt in every stroke. By 1896 he is in complete control. Paris giggled, but with an uneasiness behind the smirks.

Like his friend and master, Degas, he drew and painted the "rats" at the Opera, but while Degas focused on the beauty of form and motion and the backstage ambiance, Forain concentrated more on the sexual interplay of the rats, either victims or victimizers, with middle-aged predators or admirers. His drawing is firm, but he rarely surpassed the mere anecdote. In the 1889 drawing from his own short-lived publication, *Le Fifre*, one rat is pointing out to her hesitant friend that the two prospective companions of the evening are easy marks — "they are from the country." The title, "L'Amour à Paris," reflects his cynicism. In "A l'Opéra," however, his mood is more tolerant, his satire amused and amusing. His volunteer middle-age singers are so earnest, so sincere. They may not be starring on stage, but they are having their moment of glory backstage. Forain is refreshingly gentler here, his observation just as acute.

His captionless drawing of the woman eyeing her prospect at a café is a classic vignette of Parisian sexual interplay, her table bare, his expensively cluttered with a masterful still-life of wine bottles and cigars, her glance appraising. The line is exceptionally fine, the characterization sharp. It is a satire Toulouse-Lautrec would have relished.

Forain continued to draw cartoons for *Le Figaro* until 1924, when he was 72, but soon after the turn of the century he concentrated increasingly on his painting and print-making. In his earlier, Impressionist paintings, Forain was considerably influenced by Degas and, to some extent, Pissarro. Huysmans called his paintings of café and opera scenes "little marvels of Parisian reality and elegance." About 1900, however, he turned to chiaroscuro and grisaille, especially for two series on the law courts and on religious themes. In 1925 the erstwhile rebel was elected president of the Société Nationale des Beaux-Arts.

Untitled, **Le Courrier Français**,
May 3, 1896.
Col. Mr. and Mrs. Herbert D. Schimmel.

Maximilien Luce 1858–1941

UNLIKE HIS RADICAL-MINDED fellow artists, Luce looked like a workingman and was equally at home with laborers and artists. While the Symbolist radicals sported top hats, Luce was never seen without a shapeless felt hat. Rough in appearance, gruff in speech, wasting no words, his manner concealed a humanity and a sensibility that won him many devoted friends — Pissarro, Seurat, Signac, Cross, Angrand, Roussel, van Rhysselberghe, van Dongen — mostly fellow Neo-Impressionists. But when van Dongen began to paint "snobs," Luce distanced himself. And when his army-service friend Alexandre Millerand rose in power, Luce accused him of "betraying Socialism." Of all the artists of *fin-de-siècle* France, Luce was probably the most successful in harmonizing his life and his art with his philosophy, as Aline Dardel has pointed out.

Although he was only 13 when he witnessed a slaughter of the Communards, the scenes haunted him; years later, he painted and lithographed those memories, and his hatred of the government (and the classes he held responsible) never diminished. When anarchists were rounded up after the assassination of President Carnot in 1894, Luce was imprisoned for 45 days.

A lifelong radical, he was perhaps the most consistent contributor to the radical press. When Emile Pouget launched his anarchist *Le Père Peinard*, Luce drew the masthead; he contributed as many as 200 drawings over the years. As long as a publication was of the left, whether anarchist or socialist or trade-unionist, Luce made political cartoons for it — for *En Dehors, Le Chambard socialiste, Les Temps Nouveaux, La Feuille, Le Guerre sociale* — usually for no payment. Occasionally he did lighter cartoons for *La Vie Moderne* and other popular weeklies, for which he was paid. "Luce is everywhere," Lucien Pissarro wrote to his father.

When Luce displayed artistic talent at an early age, his father insisted that he train as a wood-engraver, to ensure a steady income. After apprenticeship, he worked for Eugène Froment for ten years, doing his engraving for newspapers while painting at night at the Académie Suisse and other ateliers. Unfortunately, his long experience as a wood-engraver seems to have inhibited him in his political drawings. In many of them the line is stiff, reminiscent of his engravings, lacking the free stroke of a lithograph. Though he was

TOP
La Vache a Lait, **Le Chambard socialiste**, April 21, 1894. Bibliothèque Nationale, Paris.
BOTTOM
Filles à Soldats, **Le Père Peinard**, Oct. 2, 1898. New York Public Library.

obviously too prolific, much of his polemical work has sharp political point and some are equally effective artistically.

"La Vache a Lait," for *Le Chambard socialiste*, strikes a familiar theme with a measure of humor and originality. "Oh, Fatherland! how they love you, these bourgeois patriots!" The simple device of drawing the farmer large dramatizes the issue and makes him vastly more important than the bourgeoisie who are drinking the fruits of the farmer's — and the cow's — labors. Here Luce combines his satirical bent with his love of the pastoral.

In "How they train Russian sailors," the ship's captain gazes out to sea while the bare feet of his "disciplined" sailors dangle overhead, their corpses out of sight. The drawing is looser, the theme understated, the impact much greater than in many of his less subtle efforts.

His emotions dominated him in the awkwardly drawn "Filles à Soldats," but the cartoon, from *Le Père Peinard*, is interesting because it is so harsh a reflection of the split that took place among many of the artists during the Dreyfus case. Luce's indignation was aroused when Forain, erstwhile Communard and radical, assisted by the cartoonist Caran d'Ache, launched the rabidly anti-Semitic, anti-Dreyfus publication, *Psst*! He portrays Forain and Caran d'Ache as prostitutes in the "Psst" bordello, with an army officer and a priest, representing the two major anti-Dreyfus forces, as clients.

"Les Chaouchs s'amusent," for *Les Temps Nouveaux*, is one of Luce's most successful cartoons, convincingly drawn, quickly grasped, symbolic. The Daumier-like, trussed-up native, inches from the life-giving water tantalizingly just beyond his reach, epitomizes the victim of the cruelty, savagery and inhumanity of colonialism. In this stark tableau, the figures of the bemedalled French soldiers outlined against the vast, isolated desert emphasize the role that the desert itself seemed to contribute to the cruelty. The casual, indifferent attitude of the seated soldier intensifies the horror. The whipping scene sketched in the background belabors the point but is incidental.

Luce contributed to the left magazines until the outbreak of World War I, when he took a neutral position and painted soldiers and casualties sympathetically. After the war, he devoted himself to painting soft landscapes, still-lifes, incisive portraits, hundreds of scenes of Paris — the streets, the crowds, the traffic, the churches, the scaffolds of construction. He was a master of the industrial landscape, of fiery furnaces, factories, men at work in steel mills or rebuilding a city. In these he merged his views and his art successfully. Many were painted in naturalist style, with traces of both Impressionism and Neo-Impressionism. Despite numerous one-man shows and accolades by the critics, his paintings sold very slowly. He was accustomed to poverty, shrugged at his lack of success, and continued to paint prolifically — 4,000 canvases before he died at 83.

Comment on entraîne les marins russes, **Les Temps Nouveaux**, July 1, 1905. Institut Français d'Histoire Sociale, Paris.

Les Chaouchs s'amusent, **Les Temps Nouveaux**, July 23, 1910. Institut Français d'Histoire Sociale, Paris.

Louis Anquetin 1861–1932

THE GIANT ANQUETIN WAS often seen with the dwarf-like Toulouse-Lautrec at the Moulin Rouge, sometimes accompanied by Emile Bernard. In his reminiscences, Sir William Rothenstein recalled that "Toulouse-Lautrec and Anquetin were at this time the two leaders among the younger independent painters. Anquetin . . . was looked on as the most gifted and promising." To Robert Sherard, writing in *Art Journal* in 1899, "The painter of whom, perhaps, the greatest things are expected . . . is Louis Anquetin."

Influenced by Lautrec, Bernard and Van Gogh, Anquetin moved from Impressionism to the new "school" of Cloisonnisme, of which he and perhaps Bernard were the founders. Based on Japanese printmaking and stained-glass elements, his paintings were compartmentalized by strong colored outlines. After a period of painting "la vie moderne," he spent months dissecting corpses in a search for anatomical details and undertook an intensive study of the masters, especially Rubens and the Baroque. "There is only one truth, and that truth is to be found in the Louvre," he declared.

Deeply involved in his research in the Nineties, Anquetin withdrew from the Paris "scene," but the Dreyfus case, among other events, pulled him into the arena of action. He contributed a drawing to a portfolio issued to raise money for the defense of Colonel Picquart, the officer who affirmed the innocence of Dreyfus. For Zo d'Axa's *En Dehors*, he created a poster which portrays many of the symbolic elements involved in the case. Dreyfus is a puppet on a child's white hobby-horse, preceded by a judge with scales tipped, a grinning military, a courtier with the face of an ass leading a blind and halt old man wearing a Napoleonic hat. In a criticism of silent fellow-artists, Anquetin shows Dreyfus trailed by an aloof artist, impervious to the panorama. A tear in the crinkled

Endehors. Poster. 23¾ x 31.
Col. Mr. and Mrs. Herbert D. Schimmel.

Drumont et Vacher, **La Feuille**, Nov. 3, 1898. (Original: Lithograph. 17¾ x 12½. Col. Mr. and Mrs. Herbert D. Schimmel.)

sheet runs through the Palais de Justice and the actors in the drama. Anquetin uses the satirist's most potent weapon — ridicule — to portray the farce of the Dreyfus trial.

When Zo d'Axa launched the occasional publication *La Feuille*, one of the most striking images was Anquetin's portrait of the anti-Semite Drumont, coupled with a convicted murderer, Vacher. In these staring faces, he brilliantly captures the malevolence of Drumont (on the right) and the out-of-control fanaticism of Vacher — two faces out of Dostoevsky. A snake wraps itself around the cross which links the two — both men had claimed God's support. Drumont's eyes are sly and shrewd, Vacher's crazed, relentlessly fixed; Drumont's mouth is thick-lipped, sensuous, Vacher's tight-lipped with hate and contempt. Opposites, Anquetin is saying, bound by their hatred of mankind.

Anquetin also drew several posters with social and political implications, including a particularly striking one for *Le Rire*, and many highly decorative drawings for *Cocorico* and other journals, but he gradually dropped his graphic work. His early promise faded. The dichotomy of looking to the past for inspiration and subject ("Another who rummages in the portfolio of the masters," commented Pissarro, who had previously praised Anquetin's work) and being part of an age of innovation — to which he himself had contributed — proved too strong for him to overcome.

— Guette! Guette! Yvon!... Nos deux cuirassés tout neufs!
— Ouais! Encore quatre cents millions de livres de pain foutues dans l'eau! Souque toujours, Paulick!

Paul Signac 1863–1935

THE EXTROVERTED PUBLICIST for Neo-Impressionism, Signac, was cantankerously contradictory. As an anarchist, he detested awards, but sought and enjoyed fame. He hated capitalism, but always lived well. Basically warm and buoyant, he was capable of violent outbursts. He was kind and thoughtful, but arbitrary. He passionately wanted freedom for everyone, but for the 26 years he was President of the Société des Artistes Indépendants, he ruled like an autocrat.

It was probably inevitable that Signac should contribute drawings to the anarchist literature, surprising that he did not do more. He was an intimate of anarchist artists Camille and Lucien Pissarro, Maximilien Luce and Henri-Edmond Cross; a good friend of Jean Grave, editor of the anarchist publication *Les Temps Nouveaux*. An optimist, he never lost faith in the ideal of a new, more civilized society; he portrayed his dreams in the naive and idyllic painting "In the Time of Harmony."

But this amorphous effort to visualize anarchy in painting was the exception. In 1891, writing in the anarchist newspaper *La Révolte*, he repudiated direct political advocacy in art: "The anarchist painter is not the one who produces anarchist pictures but the one who, without thought of gain, without desire for reward, battles with all his individuality against bourgeois and official conventions by making a personal contribution. The subject is nothing or no more than one of the parts of a work of art."

His later landscapes and seascapes depicting the beauty of nature implied that the world need not be destroyed by the rigors and ugliness of industrialization.

Direct polemical art was to be excluded from painting, reserved for the anarchist newspapers. As he said, "It would be an error, into which the most well-intentioned revolutionaries often fall, to demand a systematically precise socialist tendency in works of art, because this tendency will be found even more strongly and more eloquently among pure esthetes, revolutionaries by temperament who, departing from the beaten path, paint what they see, how they feel and unconsciously give, very often, a vigorous blow of the pick to an old worm-eaten solid edifice, which is cracking and falling apart in the same way that an old cathedral is secularized."

ABOVE
A bas les chefs, pub. no. 61, **Les Temps Nouveaux**, 1912. Institut Français d'Histoire Sociale, Paris. (Original: "Les Démolisseurs." Lithograph. 22¼ x 18. K. and W. 15. Private col.)

OPPOSITE
Nos deux cuirassés. **Les Temps Nouveaux**, Sept. 22, 1906. Institut Français d'Histoire Sociale, Paris.

"A vigorous blow of the pick…" For a booklet published by *Les Temps Nouveaux*, Signac's cover drawing, "Les Démolisseurs," portrays two muscular workmen tearing down a house. Obviously, he had much more in mind: the house — "worm-eaten edifice" — was symbolic of society. On the left the sun — anarchist symbol — sets on a collapsing society. Signac had learned much from Seurat: in the monochromatic drawing the powerful central figure is monumentally formed out of gradations of black and gray, with line used sparingly. Signac also made a lithograph and a painting on the same theme.

He maintained a long friendship with Jean Grave, occasionally contributing drawings to *Les Temps Nouveaux*. In 1907, he made this sketch of two battleships, combining his love of harbor scenes with sardonic social comment. When one of the boatmen points excitedly to "our two brand-new battleships," one of the others points out that the cost is 400 million loaves of bread. The broken line, typical of his work at that period, shows how much Signac had modified Neo-Impressionism.

For another *Temps Nouveaux* booklet, on Biribi, the notorious French hell-hole in Africa, Signac effectively understates his biting comment. In a tropical setting, vultures swoop down on the corpse of a French soldier. Only the vultures benefit from the presence of French Legionnaires in Africa, Signac is saying. Placing the body in a bare expanse renders the scene all the more poignant, the death pointless.

A lifelong pacifist, Signac reproached Grave in 1917 for supporting the first World War. "Nourished by your principles, by those of Reclus, by those of Kropotkin — for it was you who molded my outlook — I could not understand how you could accept the war. For thirty years you have been proving the opposite to me." He added that he had been unable to paint for three years because of his distress. Signac adhered to his convictions throughout his life. He was a passive supporter of the Russian Revolution and in his old age actively anti-fascist, but his support for the left was rarely expressed graphically.

Pour les Vauteurs, **Les Temps Nouveaux**, July 5, 1910. Institut Français d'Histoire Sociale, Paris.

Henri de Toulouse-Lautrec 1864–1901

WIT OR IRONY ENLIVENED nearly everything Toulouse-Lautrec painted or drew. An element of satire was ever present — satire modified by a sensibility that only rarely deserted him. Often his subjects — prostitutes, dancehall habitués and performers, circus clowns — needed no embroidery. "He was perhaps the last artist of great stature to take his subject matter entirely from the reality of contemporary life, in its most public, familiar, widely shared aspect, not from a world of his private imagination," Lorenz Eitner has written. (It was, of course, not a whole world of reality; none of the humdrum side of bourgeois society and very little of lower-class life appear in his work.)

He drew for *L'Escarmouche, Paris Illustré, NIB, Le Courrier Français*, not for the money, but to gain recognition. His silhouetted figures caught in emotional or physical dishabille obviously stemmed from Degas and the Japanese printmakers, while he in turn influenced many of the artists who made the magnificent fin-de-siècle posters. His mastery of lithography was supreme; his strong line and massing of flat color were ideal for the medium. He sketched his satirical vignettes on menus, theatre programs, book jackets, even on the soles of Misia Natanson's feet.

Fascinated by Aristide Bruant and his cabaret, Le Mirliton, he immortalized both with illustrated song sheets for Bruant and, later, with his famous posters of the singer. For Bruant's semi-monthly *Le Mirliton*, Toulouse-Lautrec contributed drawings under the names of "Treclau" or "T. Lautrec." Here, only 23 years old, he deals with one of his perennial themes, prostitution, with more satire in the caption than in the drawing. The 15-year-old girl is "oldish" to the reprobate. Already the artist's superior draftsmanship is manifest. His figures, like those of Villon, are drawn with style and elegance; he is not yet ready to distort.

"What's for breakfast?" is the bawdy caption of another, typically Lautrec-an cartoon, this one for *Le Rire*. The wash strokes at the woman's feet, seemingly random, help convey an atmosphere of riotous disorder.

When the cartoonist Adolph Willette asked him to create a poster for his new monthly magazine, *La Vache Enragée* (named after a popular slapstick farce), Lautrec took the subject literally, softened it with comic touches, and injected it with

Le Moderne Jugement de Paris, **La Revue Blanche**, supplement, June, 1894. Col. Mr. and Mrs. Herbert D. Schimmel. (Original: Lithograph. 2⅞ x 2⅜. D. 69.)

Yvette Guilbert, **Le Courrier Français**, Sept. 2, 1894. Rep. from **Yvette Guilbert**, text by Gustave Geffroy. Lithograph. 13½ x 7. D. 83. Col. Mr. and Mrs. Herbert D. Schimmel.

Le Crocodile, 1896. Lithographed menu.
12⅝ x 9⅞. D. 200.

forceful movement rare for him. His brilliant line strongly projects the flight of the fearful bourgeois, the massive power of the bull and the haplessness of the Keystone-comedy cop. He even works in two clowns as onlookers.

Caricatures came easily to him (perhaps his grotesque body heightened his sense of the grotesque) and added a dimension to his sketches of Montmartre night life. The caricatural elements in his 1894 album-tribute to singer Yvette Guilbert outraged her parents and shocked some of the critics, but most saw the humanity and dignity behind the somewhat homely features. The jet black of her gloves — her hallmark — leaps out at the viewer, yet does not distract from the portrait.

Lautrec's "Le Moderne Jugement de Paris" turns the classical theme — so dear to academic painters seeking an excuse to paint the nude — on its head. Paris is now a client in a brothel, with three prostitutes exhibiting their wares. Lautrec must have enjoyed this sardonic comment on a sex-ridden society in which he participated so much, for he included it in his album "Les Chasseurs de Cheveleurs," had it published in *La Revue Blanche* and *Le Rire* and lithographed it on a menu. He enjoyed making lithographed menus for special occasions out of ironic, improvised, on-the-spot sketches, such as "Le Crocodile." This menu was made after a trip with friends to Blois, where they had heard the story of Marie de Medici's flight. Lautrec's cousin, Dr. Gabriel Tapié de Celeyranis, is portrayed as a snake, his dealer Maurice Joyant as a crocodile, while Maurice Guibert abducts the Queen.

Whatever Toulouse-Lautrec created — whether scenes of street life, bars, brothels, cafés, music halls — whether painting, drawing, print or poster, it exudes vitality and reflects the eye of the born caricaturist.

What's for breakfast? **Le Rire**, Oct. 24, 1896.
Col. Mr. and Mrs. Herbert D. Schimmel.

Quel age as-tu? **Le Mirliton**, Feb., 1887.
Houghton Library, Harvard University.

La Vache Enragée. Poster. 32⅛ x 23⅝. D. 364. Col. Mr. and Mrs. Herbert D. Schimmel.

Tu finiras par le savoir ton catéchisme !

Félix Vallotton 1865–1925

HE ARRIVED IN PARIS IN 1882, a very poor and very young Swiss, to study at the Académie Julian and to tread the well-worn path in search of elusive fame and fortune. With only a tiny remittance from his father and a talent for graphics, Vallotton inevitably turned to the illustrated journals. They provided essential income while offering an outlet for his sense of satire, his misanthropic contempt for the bourgeois, whom he regarded as abusive and oppressive, and his growing radicalism. In the Nineties, his work appeared with varying frequency in *Le Rire, Le Courrier Français, Jugend, Pan, le Quotidien, Le Canard sauvage, l'Escarmouche* and *The Chap-Book* (Chicago). He exhibited with the Nabis and at the Indépendants; with his friends Vuillard, Bonnard and Toulouse-Lautrec, Vallotton became one of the circle around Thadée Natanson and his Symbolist *La Revue Blanche*, to which he became a leading contributor.

From 1892 to '94 he was paid 30 francs each for a series of lithographs, "Immortels," *portraits charges* of leading personalities. Although Vallotton had a reserved and sober personality, the portraits revealed a satirical bent and a sense of irony characteristic of all his graphic work. For his *portrait charge* of Pierre Loti, he dressed the popular novelist as a young girl holding a ship, dolls and a wooden cross, all iconographs of Loti's novels.

But Vallotton's forte — and for many years the principal source of his income — was printmaking, especially his remarkable woodcuts. Over a period of years he made almost 100 woodcut portraits for *La Revue Blanche* and another 53 for *Mercure de France*. His woodcuts were the most original and successful part of his graphic oeuvre. Greatly influenced by Japanese Ukiyo-e prints so popular in Paris then, Vallotton cut his blocks with a strikingly individual style, endowing scenes of everyday life with a universality.

Three series on Paris captured the city with superb irony, especially the streets and the broad variety of Parisians who swarmed on them. Many others reflected Vallotton's radical reactions to the political scene of the Nineties: the police crackdown on anarchists, the military draft, the Dreyfus case (he was strongly pro-Dreyfus), superpatriotism. "The Demonstration," which appeared in the first issue of *L'Estampe Originale*, has many of the qualities that distinguish his woodcuts. He

OPPOSITE
Tu finiras . . . , **L'Assiette au Beurre**, March 1, 1902. Private col. (Original: Lithograph. 10⅜ x 8⅛. V. and G. 63.)

ABOVE
Et celui-la? **L'Assiette au Beurre**, March 1, 1902. Private col. (Original: Lithograph. 10½ x 8. V. and G. 69.)

brilliantly evoked the panic that overcame a crowd fleeing from the police. All nonessentials are stripped; as in many of the other woodcuts, the focus is on the figures, which, in Japanese fashion, are silhouetted against the street surface and situated in the upper third of the block, with many running off the scene. It abounds in vitality and movement. Each figure, formed out of a mass in Vallotton's unique manner, is taut with fear. To stress the anonymity of the crowd, his figures have no individuality.

Vallotton's cartoons for the lighter magazines were often executed with as much care as his woodcuts and frequently with the same characteristics. In this jaunty cover for *Le Rire*, some figures are achieved by linear outline, some by primarily dark masses, cut off by the frame. The horizon has been lowered, however, and perspective is conventional. The disparate figures are held together by the massive woman in white in the center of this carefully planned tableau. The caption sarcastically laments that these idlers will never be granted the eight-hour day.

In 1902, Vallotton prepared a special issue of *L'Assiette au Beurre* on "Crimes and Punishments" — the ideal subject for his cynical, astringent outlook. He was paid 1,000 francs for the 24 lithographs, and the publisher so respected Vallotton's work that he printed them on only one side of each sheet — never done before or after in the magazine. A farmer kills a man for stealing apples, a priest vigorously spanks a child for not knowing his catechism, an old employee is fired for being 10 minutes late. In one, a poor man with torn trousers is arrested for displaying his backside. Quite possibly John Sloan had seen that one when he drew his young lady with the torn skirt being condemned for "displaying" herself. "And this fellow? He shouted 'Long live Freedom,'" states the caption of this court scene, an irony repeated in *The Masses* but which Vallotton may have taken from Daumier.

Again he achieves emphasis and drama by counterpointing a large black mass — the priest, the policemen — against a relatively small white area, thus enlarging

La Manifestation, 1893. Woodcut. 8 x 12½
V. and G. 110. Metropolitan Museum of Art.

TOP
Les pauvres oisifs, **Le Rire**, April 25, 1896. Bibliothèque d'Art et d'Archéologie, Paris.
BOTTOM
Pierre Loti, 1892. From album, **Immortels, Passés, Présents ou Futurs**. Lithograph. 8¼ x 4½. Musée Cantonal des Beaux-Arts, Lausanne.

the point of view of the victim. To the child the dark cavern of the priest's robe is huge, all-powerful, overwhelming authority; to the beaten libertarian in the courtroom, the world is made up of the gleaming buttons and dark-blue coats of *flics* — again authority and power loom as one, visually. Although they are lithographs, the thick, carved lines and the white-black interplay stem from Vallotton's woodcuts.

In the early 1900's, now married to a woman with some income, Vallotton stopped making drawings for the magazines and concentrated on painting nudes, landscapes and portraits. His facility for simplifying and flattening, so effective in his woodcuts, conflicted with more conventional elements of his painting. Thus his nudes were sometimes too statuesque.

In 1915-16, greatly disturbed by World War I, he again made a series of woodcuts, "C'est la guerre," which he himself sold. So once again the profit motive combined with social concern to produce masterful polemical art.

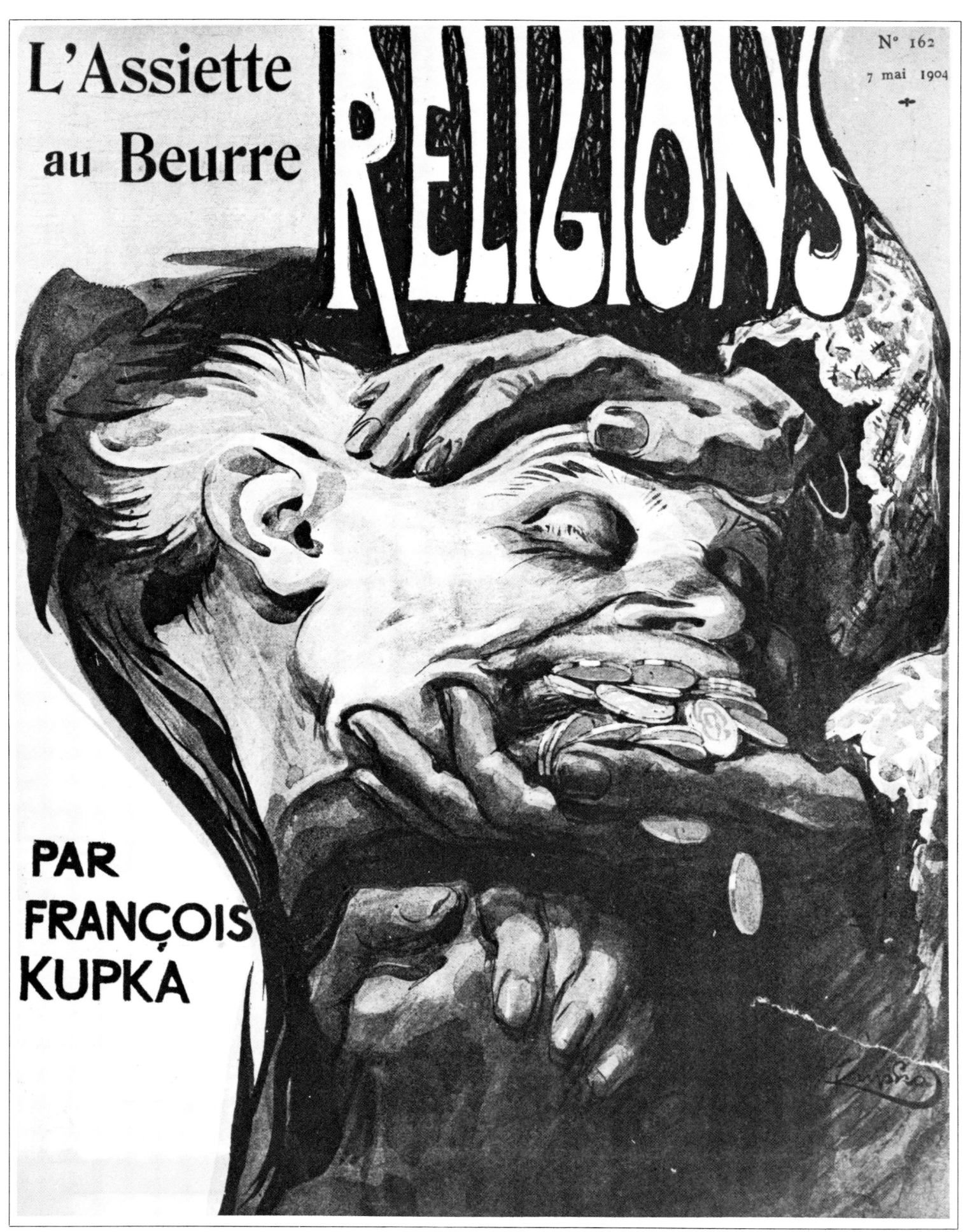

Réligions, L'Assiette au Beurre, May 7, 1904. Private col.

Frantisek Kupka 1871–1957

AMONG THE ARTISTS IN *L'Assiette au Beurre*, Kupka was one of the most virulent anti-capitalist. Anti-militarist, anti-clerical, anti-imperialist and, of course, anti-academic in his art, he detested *fin-de-siècle* France in all its political and social manifestations.

His anarchism stemmed from his background. After being a star pupil at the Prague School of Fine Arts, he took off for Vienna and Bohemia, where he lived in grinding poverty while dabbling in spiritualism and eventually suffered a nervous breakdown. At 23, he went to Paris. Incipiently radical, his individualistic philosophy gradually evolved into an ardent anarchism. While seeking his own painting style, he drew mildly satirical cartoons for *Cocorico, Le Canard sauvage, Frou-Frou, Sourire, Le Rire* and several other publications, as well as savage thrusts at the class structure for *L'Assiette au Beurre* and *Les Temps Nouveaux*. In 1900, although he continued to paint (winning a Gold Medal at St. Louis in 1902), he told a Czech friend that he was going to concentrate on graphic art because it was "more democratic."

Outstanding in the brilliant polemic art that often distinguished *L'Assiette au Beurre* was Kupka's cycle of three issues devoted to "L'Argent," "La Paix" and "Réligions," a series of drawings that won him international acclaim in leftist circles. The intensity of his emotion was transferred with such gusto to his drawing that the ordinarily lively pages of the weekly crackled with heightened vitality. Kupka rises above the banality of his subjects by his stylistic verve, his imaginative conceptions, the vigor of his thrusts.

"L'Argent" is an overwhelming encyclopedia of the abuses of money. In scene after scene, Kupka's all-powerful Mr. Rich manipulates heads of states, while the goddess of war beats her drums, and backs both sides in the Boer War — for profit. People fight, whore, gamble for money, but in true anarchist fashion, reason triumphs at the end. Three of the drawings make a mockery of Liberty, Equality, Fraternity. "Liberty" is an especially striking composi-

Liberté, **L'Assiette au Beurre**, Jan. 11, 1902. Private col.

LEFT
Untitled, **Cocorico**, March 1, 1900.
Col. Mr. and Mrs. Herbert D. Schimmel.
RIGHT
L'Argent, **L'Assiette au Beurre**,
Jan. 11, 1902. Private col.

tion. Like a huge Egyptian god, Mr. Rich sits on his golden throne, encircled by his protective puppet army, as an endless line of his workers trudge to his factories, going round and round in a circle, their lives going nowhere. An especially witty concept in "L'Argent" is his "money talks" drawing, "Le Vote Plural," his voters ranging from the three loud and influential voices of the voter with a bellyful of money to the silent one without a sou. In the background, priests pay homage — Kupka's view reflecting the rampant anti-clericalism of left-wing France at that time.

His cover, "Réligions," makes extraordinary use of art nouveau in the service of brutality, with the hands of the hidden priest squeezing coins out of the mouth of his victim. The issue is a satire on the religions of many countries — China, Japan, Turkey, Egypt, etc. — each scene drawn in the style appropriate to the country. The strongest attack is reserved for the Catholic Church. His original version was rejected by the editors as being too inflammatory.

Even in Kupka's lighter efforts, his strong draftsmanship and great talent for composition are evident, as in this art nouveau cover for *Cocorico*.

In 1906 he moved to Puteaux, where his search for a rational approach to painting absorbed his energies exclusively and carried him to his pioneering geometrical abstractions painted in brilliant primary hues. He returned to illustration and advocacy drawings only during World War I, when he also helped form a Czech regiment.

Jacques Villon 1875–1963

ALTHOUGH JACQUES VILLON received an allowance of 150 francs a month when he arrived in Paris in 1894, he was eager for financial independence. So he began drawing cartoons for the *journeaux amusants*, and for 10 years they took precedence over his painting. He was paid only 5 francs per drawing by *Frou-Frou* but 50 francs each by *Le Courrier Français* — when he could collect. This kind of work, he told Francis Steegmuller, "offers many opportunities both to observe life as it passes by and to gain insight into people's mentalities."

In search of material, he frequented the cafés, studied the street life, observed the chic rituals of the demimondaines. His "research," shared with an international triumvirate of Kupka, Gris and Pascin, was not always sociological: Villon and Kupka once celebrated New Year's Eve non-stop for three days and nights.

His mildly satirical cartoons appeared in *Le Chat Noir, Cocorico, Gil Blas, Frou-Frou*, occasionally in other publications, and especially in *Le Courrier Français*, where his work appeared until it closed in 1910. Most were amusing slices of life, occasionally sentimental, minor genre vignettes of *fin-de-siècle* Paris. A gentle quality pervades these drawings. With his sunny nature, Villon's satire was usually temperate, lacking the corrosive bite of the work of his more radical contemporaries. As Bernard Dorival has pointed out, with these journeymen works, "he acquired a rare virtuosity, a taste for drawing which approached that of the Cubists, and a sense of the human figure." Sexual themes dominated in the frothier magazines of the day; stylish and catty women played their verbal and occasional physical sexual games. In a slight departure from this formula, Villon's elderly guilt-ridden customer ("You're going to despise me," he tells the astonished prostitute) is the perfect pawn for the veteran of several hundred such encounters.

This is deadpan satire, in both caption and drawing. Villon's cartoons frequently border on illustration, with the cartoon element in the caption. His approach was much more that of painter and printmaker than of professional cartoonist. Obviously influenced by Toulouse-Lautrec and Steinlen, Villon gradually developed his own style, combining the flat washes of Japanese prints with curvilinear

Les Accapareurs, **L'Assiette au Beurre**, June 27, 1901. Bibliothèque Nationale, Paris.

Vous allez me mépriser, **Gil Blas**, Aug. 3, 1900. Institut Français d'Histoire Sociale, Paris.

outlines and short, quick strokes. Because he was absorbed in printmaking at this time, some of his drawings look like engravings, his masses resembling aquatints. They stand out in the pages of the *journeaux amusants*.

In *L'Assiette au Beurre*, for which he made 24 drawings, including one complete issue, Villon found greater scope for his drawing and his political views. The journal's full-page illustrations, often two-color, allowed more freedom of movement and breadth of conception. His radical positions, probably acquired from his friends, were revealed in *L'Assiette au Beurre* to be anti-war, anti-monopoly, anti-clergy, anti-idle-rich. But for all the asperity of his comments on society, the bite is again much greater in the caption than in the drawing, in the conception than the execution.

In "Les Associations!!!" Villon's illustrative talent flowers. His frustrated and angry priest glowers at the thought of the new "Associations" law, which dissolved many of the religious orders engaged in teaching. Behind him parades his military supporters, their power fading. The drawing typically combines dark mass with short, blunt strokes.

The graceful line of his drawing in "The Easy Life" issue belies the political impact of the contents, which were probably influenced by Kupka. Based on a quotation from Zola, it epitomizes the anarchist concept of the social structure: one of Villon's beautiful but parasitical ladies drives the workers "like domestic animals" as the peasants curtsey and in the distance smoke pours from the factories that made her rich. Villon's soignée exploiter plays the same role as Kupka's Mr. Rich; these physical opposites manifest the differences between the artists' philosophies and their stylistic approaches to the same subject. The mass of the woman's costume provides an effective counterpoint to the lighter brushstrokes of the exploited, emphasizing her affluence; but the concept is weakened by her posed look.

In "Les Accapareurs" ("The Monopolists — Make a little room for M. l'Abbé"), he uses the curve of the carriage and the frailty of the aristocrats' thin figures to accentuate the corpulence of the priest. In this instance, Villon's graceful presentation is especially fitting for his subject. It enhances the effect rather than lessening it.

In "High-Life-Tailor," Villon continues the French tradition of poking fun at Englishmen's dress. His three trouserless English sahibs, with helmet, necktie and pipe, maintain their cool dignity as they brave the dangers of the jungle. The swirl of the tropical tree reflects the art nouveau curves of the masthead.

Villon did not appear in *L'Assiette au Beurre* after 1902. Possibly he was more at home in the less ideological pages of *Le Courrier Français*. In 1906 he moved to Puteaux, partly to escape the distracting camaraderie that made serious work difficult. By 1911 he was painting his own version of analytical Cubism and joined the Section d'Or group. His preoccupation with light and color led him to dub himself a "Cubiste Impressioniste."

Des ouvriers . . . **L'Assiette au Beurre**, Feb. 15, 1902. Private col.

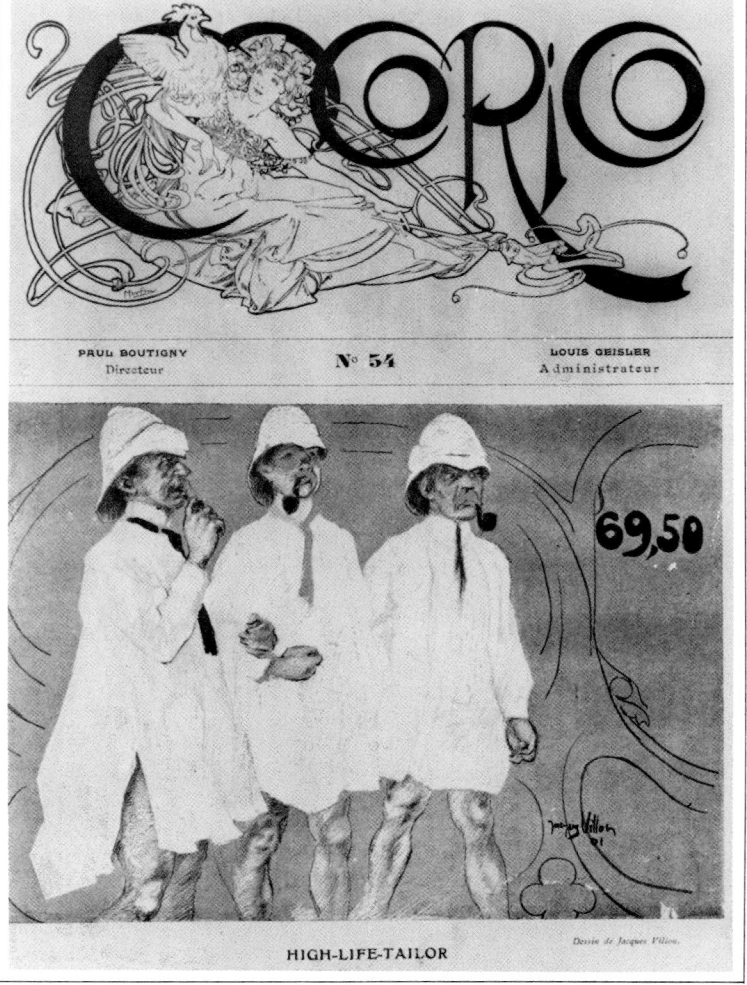

High-Life Tailor, **Cocorico**, Nov. 15, 1901. New York Public Library.

. . . *Les Associations!!!* **L'Assiette au Beurre**, May 30, 1901. Private col.

Le Péril Blanc, **Les Temps Nouveaux,** Sept. 30, 1905. Institut Français d'Histoire Sociale, Paris.

Kees van Dongen 1877–1967

IN THE TWENTIES AND THIRTIES he was the epitome of the Society Painter, a frequenter of Cannes, Deauville and the Côte d'Azur, and party host to tout Paris. He chronicled the Jazz Age in strong, often violently contrasting colors, and society women vied to have their portraits painted by him. One may wonder at the eagerness of these petitioners, for in some of his portraits there is venom beneath the glitter of the post-Fauvist surface, a barely concealed hostility; yet his victims, like those of Goya and Daumier, seemed unaware of the element of ridicule. Other portraits reveal a sensitive insight, a penetrating sympathy for his subject; he seemed to alternate between brutality and grace. His ambivalence toward women and his preoccupation with them may have stemmed from attitudes shaped in his early years in Paris.

Van Dongen arrived there from Amsterdam in 1897, wretchedly poor in the hallowed tradition. He sold newspapers, worked as a handyman at Les Halles, scraped by. His first breakthrough came in 1901 when he was assigned to illustrate an entire issue of 16 full-page drawings on prostitution for *L'Assiette au Beurre.* He made nine additional drawings with social meaning for that publication in 1901 and 1903 and then several for the anarchist *Les Temps Nouveaux,* for which he was paid nothing. It was more profitable for him to make illustrations or humorous sketches for *Le Rire, Frou-Frou, l'Indiscrêt, le Rabelais,* and, later, *La Revue Blanche,* doing what he later called "little stupidities" in order to pay his rent. He moved into the Bateau-Lavoir, became a friend of Picasso and Max Jacob, and was close to Maximilien Luce, who oriented him toward anarchism. While he fully enjoyed the Bohemian life of Montmartre, in his studio he painted with a fresh vision, his palette explosive with violently contrasting elementary colors. Intrigued by the pioneer Fauvist, Ambroise Vollard gave him a large one-man show in 1904. A year later, van Dongen exhibited at the Salon d'Automne with the Fauves, of whom Vlaminck and Derain, both anarchists, were closest to him. "The things I wanted to achieve in society by throwing bombs about would have landed me on the scaffold," Vlaminck declared. "Now I have tried to do the same thing in art, using unblended colors, as they come out of the tube. In this way I have satisfied my need to destroy, to disobey, in order to make room for a freer or more lively world than the one

Cocotte, **L'Assiette au Beurre**, Oct. 26, 1901. Metropolitan Museum of Art.

we have today." Derain likened his tubes of paint to "tubes of dynamite."

People hooted at their "rebellious" paintings, but it didn't seem to bother van Dongen. "Most of us still had more fervor than money in our pockets. Still, we were young, we laughed and sang; thanks to color, we had our little rebellion. Best of all, we had a good time being 'wild.'"

Of van Dongen's graphic commentaries, the most effective by far was the series of 16 he did for the special issue of *L'Assiette au Beurre* on prostitution, the left's symbol of a sick society. In this "Petite histoire pour petits et grands enfants," he is sympathetic to the victims of prostitution, not to the institution. Deserted, penniless, with a young daughter, his *fille* takes to the streets, is arrested, returns to prostitution ("one must live"). After she dies, her daughter takes up the mother's trade, with less justification, peddles her flesh to hosts of admirers, grows old, fades, dies violently. Van Dongen's morality tale was intended, perhaps, as a warning to the young. His drawing is often forceful, with quick slashes and broad strokes, precursive of Fauvism, though with detail he later would eliminate. Many of his drawings have the energy of speed (not of haste), instinctual rather than intellectual. The vigorous, blunt line of the finale, "Cocotte," savagely expressionistic, is not far from the powerful strokes of his later paintings. Van Dongen was paid 800 francs for his "Petite histoire." The colored drawings were auctioned in 1971 for 321,500 francs. Of the many distinguished issues of this extraordinary magazine, few equalled van Dongen's.

His cartoons for the frothy magazines, done for what they would pay him, were commonplace, reflecting his basic lack of interest. Despite his later putdown of his dallying with anarchism, power and passion marked much of his political graphic work. His anti-society drawings were thoughtful, effective, disturbing, as in "Le Peril Blanc," drawn for *Les Temps Nouveaux*. Jesus is presented as a Jewish clown with an idiot's delight as he stands triumphantly astride a world of guns and battleships. Just as his orgies of color occasionally teetered on the edge of the precipice, so did this savage conception.

LE PALAIS DE LA PAIX...

... OÙ L'ENFANT S'AMUSE.

Dessin de MARKOUS

Louis Marcoussis 1878–1941

LOUIS MARKOUS WAS 25 WHEN he arrived in Paris from Warsaw, where he had already made satirical drawings. For easy money he contributed light sketches to *Le Journal* and *La Vie Parisienne* while he studied at the Académie Julian, until he triumphantly made the Salon of 1905. Ebullient, a brilliant talker, he quickly made friends among the avant-garde artists and poets. Starting in 1907, to support himself and his mistress, he worked almost full-time for several years for the satirical journals — *Le Rire, L'Assiette au Beurre, Sourire*. Although he continued to dash out frothy anecdotal cartoons, he also began to create more ambitious, more politically sophisticated graphic commentaries. Much of this later satirical work reflected a keen grasp of the international situation, where competition for colonies seemed to be leading to inevitable conflict.

In 1908 he made a remarkable series of cartoons for *Le Rire* on the international rivalries. A young girl, labeled "Europe," is building a "Peace Palace" out of a house of cards; her toys are shells, her models for construction are weapons. In the substance of his comment and the detail and precision of the drawing, he had distanced himself from the frivolities of his earlier efforts.

In "M. Clown, Dictateur," Clemenceau is caricatured as a clown dancing his last pirouette while fighting erupts between French colonial soldiers and German soldiers dressed allegorically as medieval knights in armor, as they often were in Markous's cartoons. The drawing refers to an incident when Germans in the French Foreign Legion deserted and were defeated by the French. Markous, consistently and correctly concerned that imperialist rivalry would end in war,

OPPOSITE
Le Palais de la Paix. **Le Rire**, Oct. 31, 1908
Private col.

LEFT
M. Clown, Dictateur, **Le Rire**, Aug. 8, 1908.
Private col.

LEFT
Colloque Sentimental, **Le Rire**, July 25, 1908.
Bibliothèque d'Art et d'Archeologie, Paris.
RIGHT
Au Maroc, **Le Rire**, March 14, 1908.
Private col.

pictures Clemenceau's exultation at the symbolic "victory" over Germany as foolish. In "Au Maroc," German efforts to enforce its claim on Morocco are blocked by a taunting France, aided by a secret agreement with a Britain that did not want to see an aggressive Germany facing her across the narrow Strait of Gibralter. The Moroccans, who have no voice in their fate, silently observe. Outright cartoon has replaced caricature in this tightly conceived tableau.

But Markous did not abandon his lighter side. His classic cartoon of the couple in the moonlight ("What are you thinking of?" "The same thing you are." "Dirty mind!") has been imitated in dozens of college humor magazines ever since.

Markous met Picasso and Braque, became a close friend of Gris and Max Jacob, and at Apollinaire's suggestion he changed his name to Marcoussis when he started his career as a Cubist. He participated in the Section d'Or and dropped his cartooning about 1912.

Pablo Picasso 1881–1973

After viewing "Les Demoiselles d'Avignon," Félix Fénéon advised Picasso to devote himself to caricature. Picasso reflected that "this was not so stupid, since all good portraits are in some degree caricature." Caricature's use of accentuation may have been one of the sources for Picasso's paintings marked by anatomical distortions as well as for some of his portraits. He often employed caricatural techniques — the foreshortening in his 1920 portrait-drawing of Stravinsky, for example — for serious effect.

Picasso's oeuvre has a plethora of examples of caricature or cartoon, especially in the early years. Those reproduced here are but a sprinkling: he was a "Sunday caricaturist" only in the technical sense that most were not drawn for publication.

With moustaches in vogue in Barcelona of 1899, he sketched his friends with exaggeratedly wide handlebars. And he liked to portray them with coat collars turned up, like conspirators, which they may well have been, for Barcelona was separatist and anarchist. He burlesqued his close friend Sebastià Junyer-Vidal as bullfighter and as classically gowned rhapsodist. He parodied the Pre-Raphaelite influence on Spanish intellectuals by portraying his friend Sabartès as a "Decadent Poet." In a manner reminiscent of Bernini's spare style, he drew his lanky, thin and long-nosed fellow-painter and Parisian companion Carlos Casagemas in classic caricatural style.

He was eclectic in these early years, influenced by Toulouse-Lautrec and Steinlen, by Carrière, then especially by Gauguin and, to some extent, van Gogh. But while he learned, he laughed, despite searing poverty, as in this parody of Manet's "Olympia," with himself and Junyer-Vidal as attendants.

While he was a traditionally struggling artist in Barcelona and Paris, Picasso reacted sardonically to the abyss that separated classes. He painted the poor, the cast-off, the lonely, and he satirized in pen and ink the despised bourgeoisie. In "Caridad," his bourgeois is a bloated caricature. A series of cartoon-like drawings expressed his contempt for the self-absorbed and uncaring middle-class. His "Elegant Couple" of 1903 are proud, smug mannequins, stripped of personality, the woman's profile ovoid. In "Homunculus Attacking an Over-dressed Old Man," of the same year, there is a hint of Cubism in the face of

La belle qui passe, 1904. Pen and ink. 11⅜ x 15¾. Zervos VI, 625. Photo Galerie Louise Leiris, Paris.

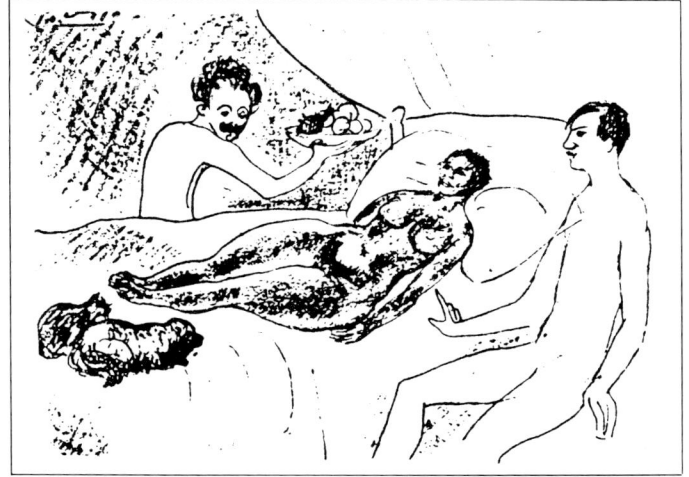

Parody of Manet's *Olympia*, 1901. Pen and ink and crayon. 5½ x 3⅝. Formerly col. Junyer Vidal. Zervos VI, 343.

Simian Self-Portrait, 1903. Pen and ink. 4¼ x 3. Museo Picasso, Barcelona.

Dream and Lie of Franco, 1937.
Etching and aquatint. 12⅜ x 16 9/16.
Col. Jacob and Frances Landau.

Personnages, 1969. Colored pencil. 10 x 12¾.
Photo Galerie Louise Leiris, Paris.

Homunculus, who is probably symbolic of the "little" people, the poor. The old man seems powerless, unresisting; if he was meant to be a symbol of the bourgeoisie, Picasso was obviously naive.

The years 1903 and 1904 were a discouraging period for him of unrelieved poverty, at times hunger, yet Picasso's humor occasionally flashed through the gloom. He caricatured himself as a monkey, drew a comic strip of Max Jacob, and satirized the eternal interplay of boys ogling girl. But his boys are pot-bellied, top-hatted leerers and the girl is plump-buttocked, her tiny dog accentuating the over-ripeness of her figure. All, appropriately, are naked. Picasso drew the last line on this familiar street scene.

Although Picasso was basically apolitical most of his life, he became engagé when counter-revolution and dictatorship threatened his native land. He chose the comic-strip form, familiar since childhood, to express his abhorrence of Franco. "The Dream and Lie of Franco," a three-part etching of a poem by Picasso and 18 panels originally planned to be published separately, read from right to left. His dictator is a loathsome monster ("an evil-omened polyp ... his mouth full of the cinch-bug jelly of his words..."), who rides forth with a crown on his dome and with the Virgin portrayed as a louse on his banner. He is finally disemboweled by a bull in the fourteenth panel. Women flee with their children from the burning houses, cry out in violent despair, lie dead. "...cries of children cries of women cries of birds cries of flowers cries of timber and stones cries of furniture ... cries of odors which claw at one another...," he wrote in a Joycean outpouring of protest.

In an extraordinary burst of vitality, at 72, the superenergetic Picasso made 180 drawings between November 28, 1953, and February 3, 1954, interpreting and burlesquing the relationship between artist and model, a literal *Commedia dell' Arte* of magnificent draftsmanship. His mistress and model, Françoise, had just

Friends with large moustaches, 1898. Crayon conté. 9 x 6¾. Zervos VI, 153.

Apollinaire. Pen and ink. Present whereabouts unknown.

left him with their two children. In his loneliness, he reflected on the nature of his art, the interplay of artist and model, the model as a symbol of sexual love and of natural beauty. He is at times serious and philosophical or only mildly ironic, at times broadly caricatural, as in a series of studio scenes where visitors fatuously admire a painting they cannot comprehend. In "The Woman Painter," connoisseur, artist and critic assume airs of knowing authority as they gaze at the obscure canvas. The smug and obviously amateurish painter is a woman, true to Picasso's sexist lexicon. The visitors completely ignore the voluptuous beauty of the nude model. Are vapid strokes on a canvas more meaningful than life itself? Picasso is asking.

As they age, most artists tend to simplify their conceptions, to eliminate detail. At 88, Picasso still drew with the strong, pure, unadorned line that had always distinguished his remarkable draftsmanship, but he also made drawings of infinite complexity, endlessly posing new challenges. His caricature of Apollinaire of 1905 is simplicity itself — a few lines and squiggles and Apollinaire is caricatured with classic economy. Sixty years later, he weaves caricatural faces out of a maze of curlicues. Unadorned line has been replaced by emphatic repetition. Apollinaire's eyes are two tiny but expressive dots, his eyebrows single lines; in these six faces, the eyes are complex, varied, equally revealing. Curving lines are even reflected in the figures of the date, 29.11.69, to serve as a background for the faces.

OPPOSITE BOTTOM LEFT
Couple in evening dress, 1902 or 1903. Formerly col. Junyer Vidal. Pen and ink and crayon. Zervos I, 147.

OPPOSITE BOTTOM RIGHT
Homunculus Attacks Over-dressed Old Man, 1902 or 1903. Pen and ink and crayon. Formerly col. Junyer Vidal. Zervos I, 150.

ABOVE
Caridad. China ink on watercolor and pencil. 10⅝ x 14½. Col. Marcelle Mabille, Brussels. Zervos VI, 438.

RIGHT
The Woman Painter, 1954. Wash. 9½ x 12⅜. Photo Galerie Louise Leiris, Paris.

Juan Gris 1887–1927

WHEN JOSÉ VITTORIANO González arrived at the Bateau Lavoir in Paris in 1906 at the age of 19, he had already drawn illustrations for the Madrid satirical journals *Blanco y Negro* and *Madrid Cómico*. Although he had gone to Paris to develop his painting (and perhaps to avoid military service), his most compelling need was to support himself in the bare studio in the tenement he shared with Picasso and others. For five years he chased the elusive franc by drawing social satire for *Le Cri de Paris*, *Le Charivari*, *Le Rire*, *Le Témoin* and especially the Barcelona journal *Papitu*. Youthful but apparently worldly-wise, he often drew sophisticated vignettes of marital infidelity, amorous intrigue, the worship and power of money. It is surprising that, though he was sober, melancholic, even pessimistic by nature, he managed to grasp and project frequently witty caricatures of the battle of the sexes. As Gertrude Stein wrote of Gris, "he has black thoughts but he is not sad." These relatively carefree sketches anticipated the leitmotifs exploited in the American satirical journals *Life* and *Judge* in the Twenties and *The New Yorker* in the Thirties.

His best work was his political satire for *L'Assiette au Beurre*, on the staff of which he worked briefly. Between 1908 and 1911, he made approximately 125 drawings for that magazine, including four complete issues. Gris's personal restraint is reflected in these drawings, which lack his colleagues' exuberant zest in attack. In emotion, they are sardonic or ironic rather than indignant, reflecting his personality. The line is usually tightly controlled, almost rigid, a style more akin to the artists of *Simplicissimus* than to those of his French colleagues. His faces nearly always lack vivacity, but if the drawings do not have the slapdash verve of those of his colleagues, he compensated with his unfailingly solid, tightly woven composition and disciplined draftsmanship. His approach was linear, reinforced by well-defined outlines, supplemented by solid areas reminiscent of Toulouse-Lautrec and Beardsley. He looked for any excuse to posit a dark mass against the detail of his controlled line, and in his later drawings he experimented with a much fuller line, like that of a woodcut.

In "The Two Classes" ("Turkey will divide her people into two classes: those who work and those who watch others work"), he makes ironic comment on

ABOVE
La Conférence, **L'Assiette au Beurre**, Oct. 24, 1908. Private col.

OPPOSITE
Les Suicides, **L'Assiette au Beurre**, Aug. 21, 1905. Private col.

the Turkish Revolution. *Plus ça change*, he is saying. Although the young Turks had succeeded in restoring the Turkish Constitution, Gris felt that the basic social and economic structure remained the same. He combines linear and geometric patterns in a manner slightly precursive of Cubism. The angles of the crossbeams and the ladders, the rectangles of the bricks, obviously interest him as much as the problem of silhouetting the figures without having them interfere with the intricate design.

He returned to the theme of Turkish independence two months later in "La Conférence," a Beardsleyan study in black and white. The Russian envoy's cynical comment to the other ambassadors that Russia would defend the territorial integrity of Turkey — until the international conference awards her a piece of it — typifies Gris's anti-imperialist sentiments.

Although the two covers by Gris — the sombre "Les Suicides" and the lighthearted "Les Aéroplanes" — contrast in subject, both share his characteristics as a draftsman: his affinity to treatment of the figure as a flat mass, with no or little effort to depict the body's form; either little interest in or inability to draw the face, and no individuality; a stiffness in the draftsmanship. Even his chiselled and cramped signature contrasts with the dash and sweep of the signatures of most cartoonists. But the mass effect is striking; both draw you immediately into the scene; his style is unique, his instinct for composition impeccable. In "Les Suicides," he is obviously intrigued by the rigid verticals of the houses to counterpoint the figures. Both make a typically sardonic point: the rich bourgeois denouncing the impoverished suicide as a "coward" and "deserter," "unworthy to live," and the frontier guards trying to cope with the new machine that makes frontier posts meaningless.

In 1912, Gris sold a painting and, according to his dealer, Daniel-Henry Kahnweiler, never drew another cartoon. But he did not make an abrupt transition. His Cubist oil painting, "The Man in the Café," 1912, is a caricatural first cousin of the pompous bourgeois in evening clothes whom he loved to satirize in *L'Assiette au Beurre*.

Les Deux Classes, **L'Assiette au Beurre**, Aug. 29, 1908. Private col.

Les Aéroplanes, **L'Assiette au Beurre**, Nov. 14, 1908. Private col.

Sir Edwin Landseer 1802–1873

LANDSEER WAS THE DOG'S BEST friend. From the age of five, he drew dogs of all breeds, shapes and sizes, as well as cows and horses. "Landseer gives his beloved animals soul, thought, poetry, and passion," Théophile Gautier wrote. The popularity of his animal paintings was enormous; he became England's best-known painter; he taught Queen Victoria to etch, was knighted in 1848, and executed many commissions for the royal family. He was a Success.

Landseer combined scientific accuracy, keenly observed anatomical detail and a genuine feeling for animal life with the sentimental anecdote and story-telling that so suited the Victorian temperament. Often the portraits of his patrons' dogs were anthropomorphic, impressing his contemporaries, but depressing his standing for posterity. A fresh look at his earlier work and especially his late paintings, such as the desolate, gruesome "Man Proposes, God Disposes," reveals what this extraordinary talent could achieve when he was not lusting after popularity.

Son of an impecunious engraver, Landseer revelled in his acceptance by England's aristocracy and literary figures. He charmed them with his stories and wit, delighted them with his pen-and-wash sketches of them. He drew for his supper and paid a price in the inevitable stress caused by his playing an ambiguous role in Society while trying to fulfill his painting commissions. He left his spoor — hundreds of witty, often satirical pen sketches of his hosts and their guests — in dozens of English country houses of the aristocracy, the great and the near-great. These deft sketches of a social scene he relished indicate that for all his basking in the acclaim of England's mighty, he reserved an objective and satirical perspective.

At times his satirical sense carried over into true caricature. His "Unidentified Knight of the Garter" captures the pomposity, the pride and the seriousness of the British gentlemen of the Empire — especially newly honored gentlemen. Be-ribboned, be-gartered and be-moustached, this solemn and earnest Colonel Blimp knows, as certainly as the sun rises, that it will never set on the British Empire.

Landseer is in an even more playful mood in "Mathews as a River God," a sketch of his close friend, the actor Charles Mathews. Hair askew, looking slightly mad, Mathews is portrayed as the epitome of the melodramatic provincial actor about to orate. The rapidly sketched caricature, with economy of line, especially in the body, contrasts sharply with the precise detail of his animal studies.

In his satirical sketch of the witty Sydney Smith, Landseer emphasizes the worldly side of the good Reverend, his portly silhouette dominant. A disapproving monk hovers in the background, upset, no doubt, by Sydney Smith's forthright condemnation of injustice, while a devil, not an angel, is suspended above. Resignation to man's failures seems to be expressed in the intelligent face of the canon of St. Paul's.

Landseer had a breakdown in 1840 and from then on suffered from ill health, hypochondria and despondency — a condition that led to occasional alcoholism, but also to thoughtful, pessimistic allegories in his paintings.

LEFT
Mathews as a River God. Pen and ink. 7¼ x 4½. National Portrait Gallery, London.

RIGHT
Unidentified Knight of the Garter. Pen, aqua ink and wash. 11⅝ x 7½. Royal Library, Windsor Castle.

OPPOSITE
Sydney Smith. Pen, sepia ink and wash. 9⅜ x 7½. National Portrait Gallery, London.

Dante Gabriel Rossetti 1828–1882

NO MATTER HOW ROSSETTI'S models differed physically, many of these "stunners," as he and his friends called them, seemed to look alike in his paintings — languid, tall, melancholic, enervated, pale to the point of anemia, yet with a touch of eroticism. In "The Annunciation," for example, his Virgin seems more sensual than spiritual.

Though romantically abstract in his approach to women in his paintings, he managed to retain some sense of the absurd about them in his caricatures, which he made occasionally for his own amusement. "The M's at Ems" is a delightful satire of life in the William Morris household. While Morris's beautiful wife, Jane Burden, sits naked and passive in the bath, the serious, intellectual husband, preoccupied as usual, pays no heed to her sensual body; never one to waste a moment, he reads aloud to her from his lengthy poem, *The Earthly Paradise*. The bored Jane, on the second of seven glasses of wine, is on her way to oblivion. There's a touch of envy here; for a time, Rossetti was in love with Jane and she was the inspiration for many of his canvases. At times he presents Morris as a man devoid of romance or passion, who views his wife as a scientist might study a specimen under the microscope.

Rossetti was a superb draftsman. If none of his paintings achieved immortality, certainly some of his drawings have, especially the portraits of his model and wife-to-be, Elizabeth Siddall. His quick, incisive line is evident in this unflattering self-portrait. Unsparingly bald and plump, he bears little resemblance to the chivalrous knights he depicted or the poet he was in word and paint. The intelligent eyes stare directly and defiantly; the sensitive mouth is scratched over as if on second thought he wanted to appear bolder. Rossetti undoubtedly meant this as a self-caricature, but he found it easier to caricature others; this bears the more direct stamp of truth.

The handsome Millais is portrayed too handsomely, uttering a favorite slang word used by the Pre-Raphaelites to express contempt for the academic practice of contrived highlighting. With a simple, firm outline, Rossetti stresses the patrician features of Millais, making him more aristocrat than rebel. The satirical sketch has prophetic insight. Within a short time, Millais the quondam rebel was to become an associate member of the despised Royal Academy and eventually one of England's highest-paid artists.

Although Millais left Rossetti's circle, Rossetti continued to influence Morris, Burne-Jones and generations of British artists whose "art-for-art's sake" stance stemmed in part from his aesthetics.

ABOVE
Sir John Everett Millais, c. 1851–1853.
Pen and ink. 7 x 4⅜. Birmingham Museums and Art Gallery.

RIGHT
William Morris presenting a ring to his future wife.
Pen and ink. 9⅝ x 11. Birmingham Museums and Art Gallery.

LEFT
Self-portrait. Pencil. 3¾ x 3.
National Portrait Gallery,
London.

BELOW
The M's at Ems. Pen and ink.
4¾ x 7. The British Museum,
London.

Sir John Everett Millais 1829–1896

FROM EARLY CHILDHOOD, success beckoned. A prodigy, he sketched his elders at seven, was admitted to classes at the Academy at eleven, and at fourteen won a gold medal for drawing the antique. His remarkable gifts were evident to everyone. And he was handsome, charming, intelligent. But he came under the spell of his fellow-student Rossetti, joined the rebel Pre-Raphaelite Brotherhood and shocked the critics in 1850 with his extremely realistic "Christ in the House of his Parents," usually called "The Carpenter's Shop." For two years he painted the best of the Pre-Raphaelite canvases; but in 1853 his uneasy period of rebellion ended.

In the same year he travelled to Scotland with his mentor, John Ruskin, and his wife, Euphemia. He fell in love with Euphemia and chastely courted her. She divorced the indifferent Ruskin and married Millais. In a few years, with family responsibilities pressing, he seems deliberately to have set out to paint in a popular vein. All intellectual and social London began to pay homage to him, and in 1896, by then a baronet, he was elected President of the Royal Academy. But today only a few of his paintings seem to have the inspiration to match his extraordinary technical gifts.

On his trip to Scotland, Millais not only indulged in discreet eye-courtship of Euphemia Ruskin but used his already prodigious draftsmanship to fill a sketchbook with caricatures of himself, his companions, the weather, the customs and mythology of Scotland. Less personal than the caricatures of Rossetti and Burne-Jones, light or humorous in tone and subject, many of them are meticulous drawings

Pre-Raphaelite sketching inconveniences in windy weather, c. 1853. Pen and ink. Photo Royal Academy of Arts, London. Col. Sir Ralph R. Millais.

rather than hasty sketches, with form and volume skillfully indicated.

Forceful shading rather than strong lines — a technique used throughout his sketchbook — creates the drunken, blissfully smiling tourist, hat askew, legs wobbly, stocking down. The strong diagonal created by the upraised arm and the table accentuates the forward thrust of the ill-fitting kilt. In "Pre-Raphaelite sketching inconveniences," a title of masterly understatement, the artist, in attempting to retrieve his umbrella and hat, is about to follow them down the rapids, while a local Scottish fisherman looks on passively. Millais superbly combines action and satirical comment. Perhaps he is apologizing for painting so little while on the sojourn with the Ruskins.

Millais's humor in these deft sketches is genteel, mid-Victorian, in the mood of *Punch* (to which he sold a sketch in similar vein on a Scottish theme). Possibly he was intimidated by the presence of Ruskin, whose portrait he was painting. In the sketchbook, he also gleefully satirized Scottish heroes, whom Euphemia admired, as well as old-master paintings discussed so intellectually in the evenings. But after this trip, Millais only occasionally made satirical drawings in his sketchbook.

In the privacy of his letters, however, he did not have to draw with Ruskin looking over his shoulder. The sketching is minimal, without detail, dealing frequently with life's little frustrations. In "Sleep at any price," again the central figure dominates, this time by strong outline — the sleepless mineralogist weighing the loss of a valuable specimen against the silencing of the offending rooster.

LEFT
Sleep at any price. Pen and ink. 7³⁄₁₆ x 4⅜. Birmingham Museums and Art Gallery.
RIGHT
The tourist's Highland reel, 1853. Pen and sepia ink. 8⅛ x 4½. Col. Sir Ralph R. Millais.

Sir Edward Burne-Jones 1833–1898

THE FRIENDSHIP BETWEEN Burne-Jones and William Morris, which lasted a lifetime, began at Oxford, affected the careers of both, and has been memorialized in Burne-Jones's deft, teasing, affectionate caricatures of Morris. Shortly after Oxford, Burne-Jones introduced Morris to Rossetti, whose medievalism was to have a permanent, though modified, influence upon both of them. For Morris, Burne-Jones designed stained-glass windows and tapestries, painted furniture and illustrated many books, in their joint endeavor to salvage the tradition of hand-craftsmanship that was rapidly being obliterated by the mass-production methods of the new industrialism. Together they revolted — Morris in his poetry and crafts, Burne-Jones in his paintings — against the philistine tastes of the Victorian bourgeoisie.

Burne-Jones's essentially linear paintings might be called "Neo-Pre-Raphaelite." Frequently allegorical, often steeped in the Arthurian legend, his paintings portray an idealized, romantic world. Against *quattrocento* backgrounds, he painted Mannerist women — tall, melancholic, ethereal. He "imagined a world without tears and laughter...," Quentin Bell has written, "in which everyone is quietly and decently sad." He escaped from the realities and horrors of industrialism into myths and fairy tales, a world of ideals that he hoped might inspire his countrymen to a loftier vision.

If there is an element of pomposity in Burne-Jones's paintings, there is none in his charming caricatures. He took particular delight in caricaturing William Morris — as Dionysus, as St. Sebastian, as an angel, as an inept husband, as an awkward skittles player.

Here, in "William Morris Reading Poetry," he satirizes his friend's notorious proclivity for intense, oblivious concentration. "Morris in Bed" portrays him as a Roman emperor, snoring musically. Perhaps

RIGHT
Self & Family. Pen and ink. 9 x 5.
Col. Mrs. Anthony J. Garner, England.

OPPOSITE TOP
William Morris Reading Poetry. Pen and ink.
4½ x 7. Present whereabouts unknown.

OPPOSITE BOTTOM
William Morris in Bed. Pen and ink. 4½ x 7.
Present whereabouts unknown.

the cobwebbed washstand is a reference to Socialist Morris as a friend of the great unwashed (but he also drew a corpulent Morris spilling out of his wooden bathtub). In "Self & Family," Burne-Jones satirizes himself exaggeratedly as the traditional struggling artist, emaciated and family-ridden.

Like Lear, Burne-Jones enlivened his letters with self-mocking caricatures, often confronted by crisis. Since his paintings are based on lofty aestheticism, it seems paradoxical that he should indulge in such lighthearted cajolery of himself and his friends. But the painter of the Arthurian legend had an impish sense of humor that had no outlet in his painting or in his role as a public figure, and found happy release in these satirical drawings. At times he revolted against the straight-jacketed morality imposed upon him: he strongly defended Oscar Wilde and in 1882 he signed a petition for the release of anarchist philosopher Kropotkin when he was arrested in France.

James Jacques Joseph Tissot 1836–1902

TO BE CARICATURED IN *Vanity Fair*, for 45 years England's leading society magazine, was a certain indication that one was Somebody in Victorian England. Most of the more than 2,500 drawings were only gentle caricatures in the Italian tradition, many of them bland portraits. But occasionally the needling was sharp; such artists as Ape, Spy, Max Beerbohm and J. J. Tissot often set a high standard for psychological insight and felicity of draftsmanship.

Of the few painters who created caricatures for *Vanity Fair*, Tissot was relatively the most distinguished. His earliest drawings — a series of sovereigns — are marked by some of the most pointed political caricaturing to appear in the magazine and reveal a strong satirical grasp of international affairs. Tissot had studied under Ingres and had appeared in the Salon before he made these drawings, probably on a visit to London.

The Sultan of Turkey is presented as a seemingly powerful ruler, holding two dolls in his arms — Greece and Egypt — while a western military figure is about to engulf him. Tissot's colored lithograph of

RIGHT
Lionel Lawson, **Vanity Fair**, Feb. 19, 1876. Colored lithograph. 11⅞ x 8⅛. British Museum, London.

OPPOSITE LEFT
Abdul Aziz, the Sultan of Turkey, **Vanity Fair**, Oct. 30, 1869 (signed "Coïde"). Colored lithograph. 12½ x 7½. Col. Clive A. Burden, Inc., Naples. Fla.

OPPOSITE RIGHT
Napoleon III, **Vanity Fair**, Sept. 4, 1869 (signed "Coïde"). Colored lithograph. 12½ x 7½. Col. Draper Hill, Detroit.

Napoleon III shows remarkable prescience. Published in September, 1869, before the outbreak of the Franco-Prussian war, the caricature depicts an aged and ailing Emperor, leaning for support on the arm of Marianne, symbol of Republican France, who is cautioning him. The frail figure symbolizes a France too weak to fight the Prussians. The reckless and feckless Napoleon disregarded the prudent admonition, plunged into war, and within a year was a prisoner.

Within a year, too, Tissot's life was drastically changed, for the boulevardier painter of chic Paris joined the Commune and fought as a sharpshooter in defense of the city. Forced to flee, he found a haven in London with his friend Thomas Gibson Bowles, the editor and publisher of *Vanity Fair*. The handsome, charming Tissot quickly gained entrée to English society and became the chronicler in paint — luscious paint — of Victorian social events, its musical soirées and garden parties. His pictorial record of the high society of the Seventies — precisely rendered, with details of clothing and accoutrements minute and accurate — is valuable for reference but too literal, too illustrative, lacking interpretation.

Tissot's mingling with the social, political, intellectual and business leaders of Victorian England gave him considerable raw material for *Vanity Fair* caricatures, of which he drew 62 between 1869 and 1877, many under the pseudonym of "Coïde." Most are character portraits rather than caricatures, but some are quite satirical. He let business tycoon Lionel Lawson speak for himself: smug, confident, exuding prosperity, unaware that his evening clothes ill fit him, he is the very model of the businessman who built industrial England. Reflecting Tissot's artistic background, this portrait of Lawson has many more painterly qualities than most of the caricatures in the magazine. Since he had training in lithography and drew directly on the stone, Tissot's drawings lost none of their nuances and his use of color was superior.

When his mistress moved in with him, Tissot withdrew from a society shocked by the arrangement. In 1882 he returned to Paris, but he could no longer find his niche. Reverting increasingly to his devout Catholic upbringing, he left for the Holy Land to portray the life of Christ, and his 360 drawings had wide appeal. Tissot died shortly after he made a subsequent series on the Old Testament.

Walter Crane 1845–1915

HE WAS THE ARTIST OF Socialism. His decorative drawings for the socialist press were displayed in factories, in workers' homes and meeting places, and were copied onto banners proudly flaunted in May Day parades. He lectured widely for the socialist cause. Shy, earnest and retiring, he was no fire-eater. Socialism was to come through education, not revolt, he believed.

His paintings often reflected the high idealism, the iconography and the style of his political drawings. As Isobel Spencer has pointed out, Crane believed that the symbol and the parable he used in his cartoons for the socialist press should also be employed in painting as a means to express strong feeling and poetic conception. With his Victorian conscience, he believed that art should have a lofty, noble aim — and that, of course, was his weakness as a painter. Although his color sense was impeccable, his line always expressive, his feeling for decoration instinctive, intellect rather than inspiration was the driving force behind his art, and though he tried to reach the heights, he rarely climbed higher than the middle slopes. Mythology, allegory, classical themes abound in his paintings, greatly influenced by Botticelli, Puvis de Chavannes and especially Burne-Jones. If his female figures are not always convincing, it is not surprising, for his beloved but Victorian-prudish wife insisted that he use only male models.

A disciple of William Morris, his mentor in both socialism and the crafts, and one of the founders of the Arts and Crafts Society, Crane designed wallpapers, textiles, pots, tiles, and stained-glass windows, and he illustrated some of Morris's fine-press books. His influence was greatest as an illustrator of children's books. For generations, children on two continents were delighted by his meticulously drawn animals, the flowing line of his fairy figures and his chivalrous knights and ladies.

Crane drew political cartoons for the socialist press — typically, for all factions — from 1884 until his death, in 1915. They appeared in *Commonweal, Justice, Clarion, Black and White*, among others. He was unique among nineteenth-century British painters in his commitment to political cartooning for a cause. In propaganda art, his use of allegory and symbolic female figures was unusual, his cartoons making a stunning contrast to those of his more realistic French contem-

THE STRONG MAN: A CARTOON FOR LABOUR DAY
MAY. "Yes, there can be no doubt about your strength if you can support all those; but don't you think it's time to take a holiday?"

OPPOSITE
Mrs. Grundy Frightened at her own Shadow, **Commonweal**, May, 1886. From **Cartoons for the Cause**.

ABOVE
The Strong Man, **Justice**, May, 1897. Ibid.

poraries. Women in classical flowing robes do not seem the stuff of propaganda. Yet they were surprisingly effective in his time; his audience was conditioned for his moralistic, high-flown approach. "The Strong Man" is typical of his annual May Day cartoons for *Justice*. Although Queen May looks like an ingenue, Labour is vigorously drawn and the three capitalist symbols were simplistic enough to gain a caustic jeer from the approving British workman for whom they were drawn.

In "Mrs. Grundy frightened by her own Shadow," Crane's woman capitalist uses Parliament to beat back the simple requests of the unemployed. With the enthusiasm of a new convert, he tries to convey too many messages, so that his point is blunted. In a cartoon drawn for the American magazine *The Comrade*, "The Capitalist Vampire" is sucking the life blood of Labour, but the always optimistic Crane has his angel trumpeting the coming of a new order. Crane's audience was international. He drew cartoons for both American and French magazines, including *L'Assiette au Beurre* and *La Revue Blanche*, and lectured widely in the United States.

But he was not always the polemicist in his drawings. Like the Pre-Raphaelites, he often stepped down from his lofty pedestal to satirize himself or his friends, as in "Beset by beasts," sketched at Hazelford on holiday.

A socialist to the end, he wrote John Galsworthy in 1911 that "my chief hope for the cessation of war . . . lies in the breakdown of the capitalist system and the adoption of socialism." Still optimistic despite World War I, shortly before his death he drew a cartoon expressing his faith in a post-war United States of Europe.

OPPOSITE
The Capitalist Vampire, **The Comrade**, Oct., 1903. **Ibid.**

BELOW
Beset by Beasts at Bassen-Thwaite, 1870. Pen and ink, 4⅜ x 7. Houghton Library, Harvard University.

Walter Richard Sickert 1860–1942

LIKE SEVERAL OF THE ARTISTS presented here, Sickert was enigmatic and contradictory, "a born chameleon," in Denys Sutton's phrase. He was tall and handsome, very witty, full of quips and songs, aristocratic, an elegant dandy, the familiar of the high and mighty. Yet he was subject to fits of depression, scorned high society ("We have a use for the drawing room — to caricature it," he wrote), loved the atmosphere of music halls (as a youth, he spent three years on the stage); at one time, he worked in dingy studios in squalid corners of London and painted lower-class domestic scenes in somber colors. He was outspoken against exploiters of the poor, yet he maintained an aristocratic stance against the poor who dressed like the rich.

His father was a Danish painter who, before he moved to England, worked for years on the leading German humor magazine, *Die Fliegende Blätter*, to support his family. From him, Sickert inherited a love for the German cartoonists Wilhelm Busch and Adolph Oberlander, and all of his life, like his friends Degas and Pissarro, he collected the work of Charles Keene and other *Punch* artists. When he separated from his wife in 1897 and lost her financial support, he took on what work he could find, including a commission for three caricatures for *Vanity Fair*.

The portrait of George Moore is slyly satirical. Critic, essayist, hanger-on and misinterpreter of the Impressionists, Moore is presented as a genial gentleman in morning coat and striped trousers. But his collar is off-center, his coat too short, his trousers wrinkled, his moustache and famous red hair dishevelled. The youthful insouciance of Manet's portrait has been replaced by self-conscious middle age.

In "Max Beerbohm," Sickert uses the conventional caricatural device of enlarging the head and reducing the body. He exaggerates the piercing sharpness of the eyes, reduces the hairline, accentuates touches of dandyism. "Max" had only recently begun to enliven the pages of *Vanity Fair*.

Sickert's later sketch of Roger Fry (which he also made into an etching) wittily presents the advocate of Post-Impressionism as a knight, his hair shaped like a helmet, a smiling, confident warrior, with ruler poised like a lance. The satire is almost affectionate, even though the two were to have strong artistic differences.

Sickert was only 22 when he caught Whistler's eye and became a pupil of "the Master." Later he was influenced by Pissarro and especially by Degas, the latter a friend until Degas's death. Sickert's style was fluid, undergoing changes as he developed his own insight. He painted landscapes, portraits and architecture, but his chief concern and greatest contribution was the portrayal of the human comedy as played out in drab lower-middle-class bedrooms.

OPPOSITE
George Moore ("Esther Waters"), **Vanity Fair**, Jan. 21, 1897 (signed "Sic").
Colored lithograph. 12½ x 7½.
Col. Clive A. Burden, Inc., Naples, Fla.

LEFT
Roger Fry Lecturing. Pen and ink. 6¾ x 3¾.
London Borough of Islington Libraries.

RIGHT
Max Beerbohm, **Vanity Fair**, Dec. 9, 1897.
Colored lithograph. 12½ x 7½.
Col. Clive A. Burden, Inc., Naples, Fla.

Lyonel Feininger 1871–1956

ALTHOUGH LYONEL FEININGER was only 16 when he left the United States for Germany in 1887 and did not return until he was 65, his formative years in America profoundly affected the concepts and contents of his comic strips, of some of his social and political cartoons, and eventually aspects of his paintings.

"High houses," which to a child seemed like today's skyscrapers, giant-adults, sinister locomotives peering into the night, bellowing ships in the harbor, anthropomorphic trees, rocks and clouds that were at one time the companions of a lonely child — these ghost-ridden memories became the iconography of his comic strips, transmuted by his gift for fantasy.

When he was nine, he played the violin in concerts with his German-born father, who expected his son to become a musician. But when he left the United States, the young Feininger enrolled in art school instead, studying art for six years in Germany and Paris. From the beginning, his talent for cartooning offered him a measure of artistic expression and a potential living. At 25, he became a featured political and social cartoonist for *ULK*, the Sunday supplement of the influential *Berliner Tageblatt*, and also soon began to contribute to *Lustige Blätter*, *Narrenschiff* and other German newspapers and magazines. Some of the early cartoons were drawn in the German comic-book tradition of greatly distorted faces, whimsical comments on the bourgeois comedy of manners. Gradually he became stylistically more individual and more forceful in his comments upon militarism and world politics.

In "Teddy's Victory Cry," drawn

OPPOSITE
The Kin-der-Kids, **Chicago Sunday Tribune**, April 29, 1906. Private col.

LEFT
Panel from Wee Willie Winkies World, **Chicago Sunday Tribune**, Nov. 11, 1906. Museum of Modern Art, New York.

for *Lustige Blätter*, he captures Roosevelt's vigor and gusto as he celebrates his presidential victory of 1904, triumphantly exhibiting the scalps of Judge John Parker, whom he defeated, and of his political enemies, William Randolph Hearst and William Jennings Bryan. Roosevelt's exuberance, booming joviality and jingoism are all portrayed in this superior political cartoon.

An assignment from the *Chicago Sunday Tribune* in 1906 to create two comic strips brought liberation from the daily drudgery of political cartooning and enough freedom to allow him to begin painting seriously. He left for Paris, where he drew the strips as well as his most sophisticated social cartoons for Paul Iribe of *Le Témoin*, and attempted his first oils.

Feininger's two comic strips ran for only six months, but elements of his whimsical nonsense and touches of fantasy were to have a lasting influence on American comics. "Wee Willie Winkies World" is one of lyrical fantasy in which clouds huff and puff and smile benignly and trees frighten or are themselves terrified. Humor and melancholy and a little fear are intermingled. A few months' stay in the rural Connecticut village of Sharon when he was young had brought him close to nature, with its wonders and terrors for an imaginative child. In the panel, Wee Willie is tiny indeed (his "Uncle Feininger" was well over six feet tall) as he looks out to sea and watches the sailing vessel blot out the sun. Nineteen years later, in one of his greatest seascapes, the comic strip motif has become a painting, *Blue Cloud*, where a figure, infinitesimally small, gazes at a modified Cubist sea and clouds.

By contrast, "The Kin-der-Kids" is full of adventure and excitement. Some of the stylistic eccentricities that distinguish

LEFT
Theddys Siegesgeheul, **Lustige Blätter**, 1904, no. 7. Private col.

RIGHT
Wee Willie Winkies World, **Chicago Sunday Tribune**, Sept. 30, 1906. Private col.

OPPOSITE
Paris (Moltke-Harden), 1908. Pen and ink and watercolor. 10½ x 8½.
Col. Andreas Feininger.

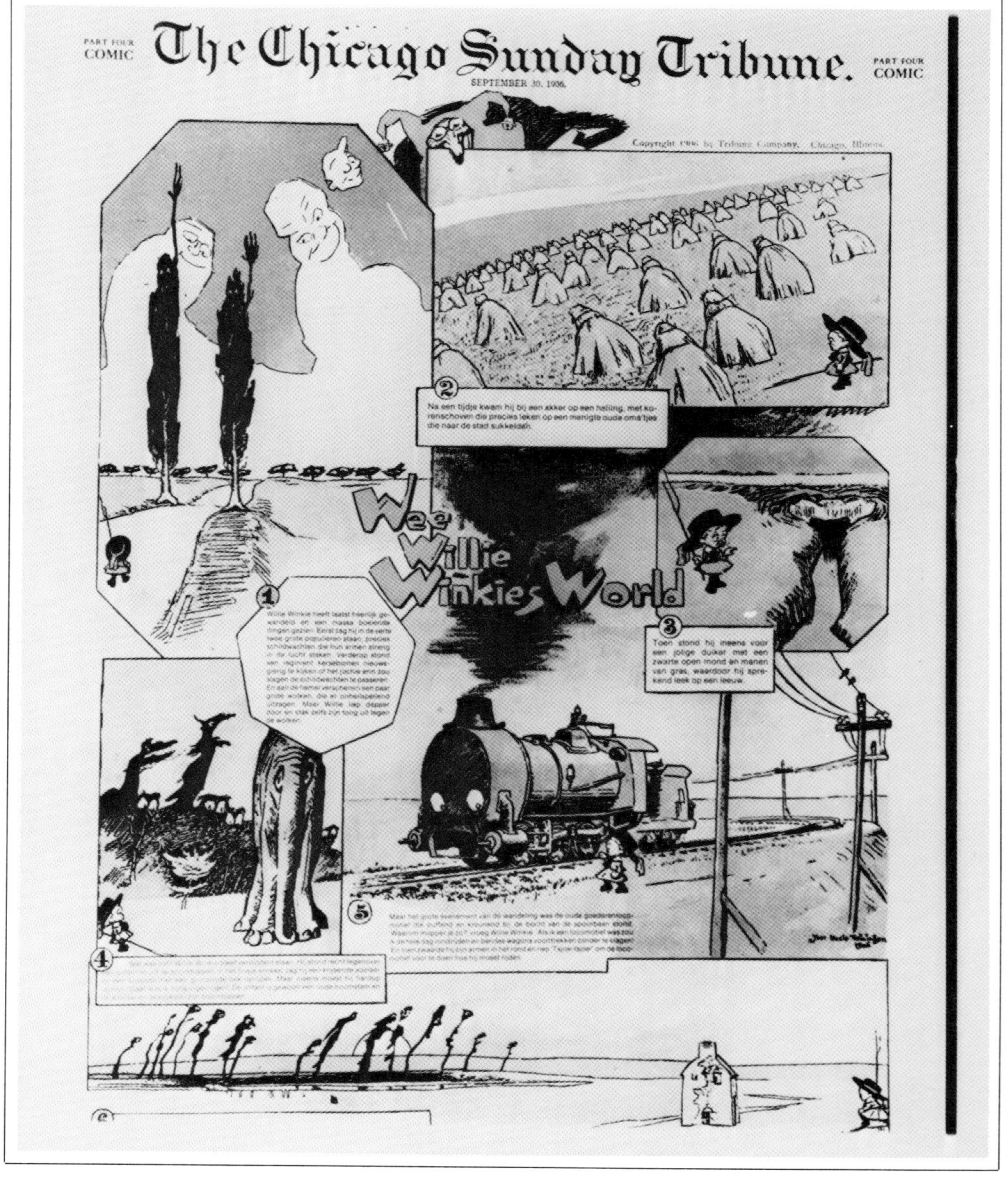

EXACTITUDE

— Où allons-nous ?
— Je n'en sais rien.

his paintings are foretold in the details of his strip: lines and planes are accented in many panels, adults are exaggeratedly tall, houses are often boldly geometric, the angularities of roofs magnified.

To emphasize the point that the separate worlds of children and adults are unbridgeable, Feininger often placed the grotesquely tall adult in the center forefront of the cartoon, as in "Le Prévoyant Fraudeur" (The Prudent Schemer), done for *Le Témoin* in 1907. The device was carried over into his oil paintings, as in "Town Hall in Swinemunde" of 1912. The flat patterns and acute angles stem directly from his cartoons. Feininger later remarked, "I am far from underestimating in my development the very important years which I spent as a draftsman for 'funny papers.' "

He drew from the child's angle even more dramatically in "Paris (Moltke-Harden)." The shrunken heads and enormously elongated bodies may also represent his contempt for the Parisians lapping up the latest gossip in the battle between Maximilian Harden's *Zukunft* and the men around Kaiser William II, especially Chief of Staff Moltke. *Zukunft's* criticisms were gleefully reprinted in the French press.

Huge adult bodies with empty minds and empty lives were the theme again of "Punctuality," based on an old joke: "Where are we going?" "I don't know." "Then, let's hurry up."

After many years as Bauhaus artist-in-residence, he returned permanently to the United States in 1937, residing a few miles from the Connecticut village where his first direct encounter with nature had made so indelible an impression.

OPPOSITE
Punctuality, **Le Témoin**, 1907. no. 30. Private col.
Le Prévoyant Fraudeur, **Le Témoin**, 1907, no. 30. Private col.

Pascin 1885–1930

Musical Evening, c. 1906. Chalk, pen and ink. 8½ x 12½. Israel Museum, Jerusalem.

The Pillar of the Family, **Simplicissimus**, Oct. 15, 1906. Private col.

BORN JULIUS PINCAS IN A SMALL Bulgarian town, he was of mixed Serbian, Italian and Spanish-Jewish origin. A precocious youth, at 16 he became the friend of a bordello madam in Bucharest, gaining background for many of his drawings and probably too early an exposure to life; at 18, in Munich, he was drawing for *Jugend* and *Simplicissimus*, paid 400 marks a month by the latter journal, although they did not publish his work until he was 20. He signed his caricatures "Pascin," an anagram for Pincas. The restless youth was soon off to Paris, where he quickly became part of the Dome group. At only 22, he had a one-man show at Cassirer's gallery in Berlin.

Always fleeing his background, known simply as "Pascin," without first name, he was emotionally as well as physically rootless all his life. He returned to Bucharest only for his mother's funeral. To escape the Bulgarian draft in 1914, he fled to New York, where the Armory Show of the previous year had gained him some attention. He wandered through the southern states and the Caribbean, obtained U.S. citizenship in 1920 and almost immediately returned to Paris, travelling frequently to the Mediterranean countries. Paris was his base, if not his home. There he exhibited frequently and again became the center of an artistic circle; but he plunged into excesses and never escaped from his isolation.

Dark and brooding, cynical, disconnected, yet with flashes of wit, he was slender, with an over-sized head and sensual lips, and, in derby hat and dark suit, was always respectably dressed, as if to compensate for the darker impulses, the time spent in brothels. As André Warnod recalled, "He was both attractive and repellent at the same time." When money came, it flowed quickly. He hungered for acceptance.

Woman was his obsession. Using opalescent colors and paint thinned almost to a wash, he captured the glow of flesh, the beauty even of the misshapen. Most of his drawings and shimmering paintings of Montmartre girls, models, brothel inmates were objective, non-committal, sensitively projected, with a tinge of eroticism.

A brilliant draftsman, Pascin drew incessantly, with matchstick, pencil, or whatever was at hand. From the beginning, his sardonic personality was at home in caricature, in wryly bitter comments. For *Simplicissimus* he made 82 drawings which appeared from 1905 to 1929. In "Rumanian

Folk Song," the young girl, like a lamb to the slaughter, is being brushed and made beautiful for her new career, while her experienced co-worker looks on critically. The grotesque characters at right and left seem to have stepped right out of a German comic strip, their earthy cynicism and ugly faces contrasting sharply with the pale youth of the novitiate. He was only 20, but the mordant tone, the skillful modeling coupled with awkward lapses, the unfailingly observant eye, were life-long characteristics, although he gradually abandoned the *Jugendstil* style.

Many of his early drawings were derisive caricatures of family life, perhaps because he had none of his own. In "Musical Evening," boredom prevails, the conceptions are cruel, but there is a touch of pathos also. The brothel violinist has graduated to bourgeois cellist. He managed to make the male musicians and audience both grotesque and human; the women simply wait listlessly for the evening to be over.

In "The Dirty Joke," the brilliant young Pascin pillories the German bourgeois with masterful line as effectively as Grosz did at a much more mature age. The snickering and leering of the fat and thin bourgeois, so respectably dressed, can almost be felt physically. The whiplash of "The Family Support" is in the caption. A pleasant domestic scene: Grandma in bed playing with granddaughter's dolls, mother casting a proud eye at beautiful daughter. The caption: "Well, Mitzi, now what do you say? They've jailed Emil for a year for pimping." "Thank God, one less to feed." At 21, Pascin already reveals his alienation from family life, his obsession with prostitution — and his remarkaby sensitive line.

In the Twenties, Pascin's expressive line became nervous, more disquieting, perhaps as his life did, although he held several exhibitions and illustrated many books. In the fall and winter of 1927-28, he came back to the United States to avoid losing his citizenship, but quickly returned to Paris. In 1930, an exhibition at the Georges Petit gallery in Paris was criticized. He brooded, and on June 2 he hanged himself, fulfilling his oft-repeated statement that an artist should not live beyond 45, for he must have achieved his peak by then. On the day of his funeral, all Paris galleries closed. The next year, a Pascin exhibition at the Downtown Gallery in New York was reviewed favorably.

TOP
The Dirty Joke, **Simplicissimus**, Sept. 19, 1905. Private col.
BOTTOM
Rumanian Folksong, **Simplicissimus**, May 2, 1905. New York Public Library.

Die Pleite

40 Pf. 1. Jahrgang, Nr. 6   Der Malik-Verlag, Berlin-Leipzig   Anfang Januar 1920   40 Pf.
Herausgeber: WIELAND HERZFELDE

Kapital und Militär wünschen sich:

„Ein gesegnetes Neues Jahr!"

George Grosz 1893–1956

UNTIL HE WAS FORCED TO flee Germany in 1933, George Grosz was the satiric voice and critical conscience of the Weimar Republic. Social commentary and anti-establishment behavior were his life's blood, yet his involvement with problems attacked by satirists throughout the ages — militarism, religious hypocrisy, dictatorship — and his adherence to socialist principles did not produce arcane polemical art. Rather, Grosz was innovative as a caricaturist, cartoonist, printmaker and painter.

George Ehrenfried Grosz was born in Berlin. He studied drawing when he was only five years old. His early models — which influenced his work well into adulthood — were Wilhelm Busch and American "penny dreadful" magazines. In his early teens he came under the influence of *Jugendstil*, the prevailing cartoon style of the day. He emulated Lyonel Feininger, whose work he saw regularly in *ULK*, the humor supplement of the *Berliner Tageblätt*, and at seventeen sold his first cartoon to this journal. He soon abandoned *Jugendstil* in favor of a more classical drawing style. His focus changed as well, to images of society in turmoil — among them, unemployment lines, street fights and beleaguered workers. Later, under the direct influence of Pascin, Grosz rendered the underbelly of the human comedy with an intimacy not usually practiced by cartoonists of his time. In his early twenties, inspired by Alfred Kubin's grotesquely satiric illustrations, Grosz's graphic "signature" developed.

His experiences as a soldier in World War I etched an everlasting scar and further crystalized his need to cry out through satire. Like his contemporaries, Max Beckmann, Ludwig Meidner and Otto Dix, Grosz employed a formal Expressionistic graphic vocabulary in order to depict personal despair at the horror of war. His first drawing and poem on this theme appeared in 1915 in the Expressionist journal *Die Aktion*. His graphic commentaries were firmly in the modes of Goya and Daumier.

The work he produced immediately after the war was rooted in revolutionary fervor. Art had no higher purpose than to serve the Cause. In this light he saw Cézanne and Picasso as dull painters of sentimentality; he preferred Ensor and other moralist artists. Although Grosz created some striking canvases, including the bitingly critical "Germany, a Winter's Tale" (1917–19), drawing was his

Ludendorffs Rückkehr

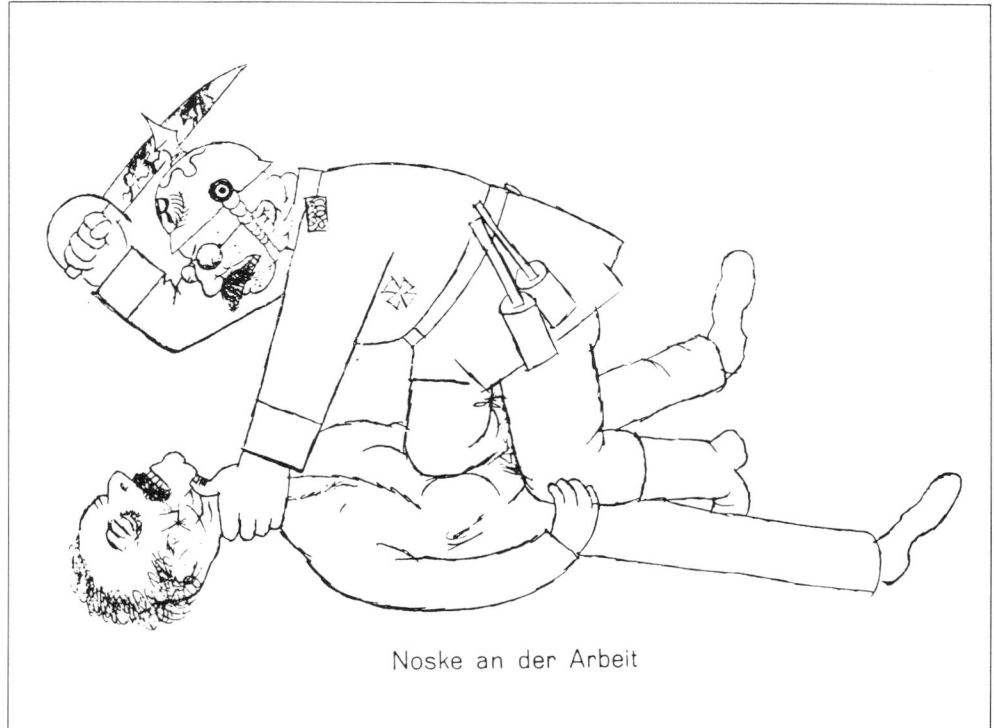

Noske an der Arbeit

OPPOSITE
Kapital und Militär wünschen sich: „Ein gesegnetes Neues Jahr!" **Die Pleite**, Jan. 1920. Private col.
TOP
Ludendorffs Rückkehr. **Die Pleite**, 1919 (Nr. 1, 1. Jahrgang). Private col.
BOTTOM
Noske an der Arbeit. **Die Pleite**, 1919 (Nr. 1, 1. Jahrgang). Private col.

OPPOSITE
Die Deutsche Pest. **Die Pleite**, Dec. 15, 1919. Private col.

RIGHT
Prost Noske — das Proletariat ist entwaffnet! **Die Pleite**, April 1919. Private col.

preferred medium between 1917 and 1925.

In 1918 his association with Richard Huelsenbeck and the Berlin Dada group brought him closer to the ideal of marrying art and politics. Moreover, this was a movement which could bring him closer to polemical art and enable him to show his outrage at bourgeois folly.

As a Spartacist (member of the German Communist party), committed to the socialist revolution, Grosz was deeply involved with the revolutionary events of 1918–19. He was a prolific participant in the Malik Verlag, the socialist publishing firm, producing scores of posters for demonstrations and satirical illustrations for critical journals such as *Der blutige Ernst (Deadly Earnest)*, *Die Pleite (The Struggle)*, and *Der Gegner (The Advocate)*. "I love newspapers," he said. "Of course, they are far more important than books for propagating ideas because far more people read the papers." The cartoons reproduced here were done for *Die Pleite* in which he abandoned his critical stance for more agitational messages. All are drawn with Grosz's characteristic hard-edged, scratchy lines, and all employ his profound hatred of capitalism and militarism — the two forces responsible for Germany's turmoil. In "Capitalism and the Military wish one another 'A Blessed New Year,' " the executed are bound even closer together in death. In "The German Disease," the Freikorps soldier, the violent tool of the monarchists and militarists, is caricatured with emblematic severity. In "Ludendorf Returns," the Weimar officials betray the Republic to the enforcer of law and order. In "Noske and the Worker," the chief of security callously and brutally restores order. "Mayday in a Big Prison" is an attack on the Republic's crackdown on communist and socialist sympathizers. The stiff caricature in the foreground, recalling the Freikorps cartoon, is a virtual exclamation point in this tableau on German justice. None of these cartoons has the allegorical

Prost Noske! — — das Proletariat ist entwaffnet!

Die Pleite

40 Pf. 1. Jahrgang, Nr. 5 Der Malik-Verlag, Berlin-Leipzig 15. Dezember 1919 **40 Pf.**
Herausgeber: WIELAND HERZFELDE und GEORGE GROSZ

DIE DEUTSCHE PEST

quality of so many of Grosz's works, for here he is creating decidedly iconographic imagery for his Cause. Grosz also produced numerous portfolios, such as "Gott Mit Uns" ("God with Us"), which was confiscated within the first few months of publication for being anti-military. For his subsequent "Ecce Homo," he was brought to trial for pornography.

During the mid-Twenties his style changed markedly, becoming soft rather than hard-edged, realistic rather than expressionistic. He was transformed from the Spartacist agitator to the bourgeois moralist. He gave up his scratchy crow-quill pen for the soft-pointed pencil. He drew scenes from life rather than cartoons. And, in the manner of the *Neue Sachlichkeit (New Objectivity)*, he employed "synthetic realism" in portrait painting and historically critical images. However, with the specter of Hitler looming ever more darkly, Grosz soon used the pen again, like a lance, to strike piercing blows.

In 1928 he was accused and found guilty of blasphemy for "Shut up and Soldier on," a drawing of a Christ figure on a cross wearing combat boots and a gas mask, for the portfolio entitled "Hintergrund" ("Backcloth"). Forced out of Germany in 1933, Grosz went to the United States to be cared for by his friend, humorist Alexander King, who offered him a sinecure on the satirical magazine *Americana*. Grosz could draw anything that struck his fancy. He opened a studio for teaching landscape painting and began to teach at the Art Students League. After the war he painted some horrific testaments to conflict, and later created his depressing Black Hole series. He also did exquisite watercolors of pastoral scenes and some excellent book illustrations for the Limited Editions Club. But his critical work was past. He could not work up the passion to criticize America with the same vehemence with which he attacked Weimar. And, though he sometimes tried, most of Grosz's later cartoons were conceptually uninspired and emotionally flat.

Maifeier in Plöltzensee. **Die Pleite**, May 1, 1919 Private col.

Maifeier in Plötzensee.

John Sloan 1871–1951

JOHN SLOAN'S FORMATIVE YEARS spent working on Philadelphia newspapers had a lasting effect on both his painting and his political cartoons. For the *Philadelphia Inquirer* and later the *Philadelphia Press*, he made sketches for the feature pages and the Sunday supplements, some spot-news drawings and, especially, many illustrations from scenes of daily life. He even drew a comic strip.

His most successful paintings were those of humanity observed in New York — the regulars at McSorley's Bar, shopgirls on Sixth Avenue, elderly Fifth Avenue snobs in their carriages, the comings and goings at the old Lafayette Hotel, women drying their hair, a man flying pigeons on a roof, riders on the Staten Island ferry. Although he did not settle in New York City until 1904, when he was 33, he rapidly became the superb visual reporter of New York life in the first decade of this century, capturing in both paintings and etchings, in grays and tones, by day and night, the vitality of homey incidents, the sweep and variety of the daily scene. Rarely profound, sometimes romanticized and sentimentalized, his urban paintings have, nonetheless, a sensitive empathy that transcends mere reporting. He was the outstanding painter of the Ashcan School.

Only occasionally did social comment creep into his painting. His polemical art was confined to drawings for the *Socialist Call* and then for *The Masses*. Sloan's radicalism was contradictory. Although the masthead on *The Masses* — to which he devoted several years as art director — bore the slogan, "A Revolutionary and not a Reform Magazine," Sloan was a reformer and by no means a revolutionary. He wrote in his diary: "I am rather more interested in the human beings themselves than in the schemes of betterment." He spent a half-dozen years as an active socialist, humanistic rather than radical, with a burning sense of indignation at injustice but no commitment to class struggle. Although he satirized the rich, he did not bludgeon them; he felt for the poor, but often presented them as happy and carefree in their poverty.

Many of Sloan's 53 drawings for *The Masses*, executed in illustration style, had an anecdotal quality and were intended to express human sympathy, not to make a crushing political point. Influenced by Daumier, Forain and Charles Keene, his drawings were much more detailed than the average political cartoon and relied on

National Association of Manufacturers, **The Masses**, Oct., 1913. Col. Ben Goldstein.

"Circumstances" Alter Cases, **The Masses**, May, 1913. Col. Ben Goldstein.

light-and-shade contrasts for emphasis and tension. The editors often added captions to give the drawings a sharper political effect, an action that Sloan and several other artists disputed (somewhat disingenuously, since he himself had occasionally added captions). He resigned from the staff in 1916, when he felt that the magazine had become too doctrinaire and the editor had too much power over the artists. " 'Circumstances' Alter Cases" may well have been one of these — a typical Sloan slice-of-life illustration, made into a pungent political cartoon by the caption. "Draw with human kindness," he advised in Gist of Art, "with appreciation for the marvels of existence. Humanism can be applied to drawing chairs and cobblestones. Look at the world of Daumier."

Despite Sloan's optimism, at times his indignation propelled him into a radical stance. After the Ludlow (Colorado) Massacre, where striking miners and their families were shot down in their tent encampment, Sloan drew this impassioned cover for The Masses. The strokes are bold and emphatic; a single figure stands out, giving the drawing a sharp focus, although the net effect is painterly. And, in a departure from his usual philosophy, his miner is striking back, with violence, in this powerful graphic commentary.

When the Congress talked of investigating the National Association of Manufacturers for undue influence, Sloan pictured the N.A.M. as a massive primordial creature in his secure cave, totally ignoring the pinprick of the investigation. From his etchings he employed the technique of crosshatching to depict form and the play of muscles on the monstrous giant. Sloan is much more successful here in modelling volume than he is in most of his drawings for The Masses. His Masses work lacks the trenchant observation of his earlier etchings, some of which have the amused humanity of a Daumier, although in all of his draftsmanship there is not a semblance of the elegant line Daumier possessed.

Sloan's contributions to The Masses bristled with indignation at times but more often enlivened the magazine with wit and occasionally with humor. After the Armory Show of 1913, which he helped organize, he drew for The Masses "A Slight Attack of Third Dementia," his amused and amusing comment on the strange new phenomenon of Cubism. It may seem today to be heavy-handed and provincial, but it is gentle joshing, drawn "with human kindness." Actually, the Armory Show's exposure of Fauves and other Post-Impressionists greatly expanded his horizon as an artist.

After he resigned from The Masses, his social observations were confined to the gentle satire of the genre scenes he sketched in his prints, and about 1929 his prints dropped comment altogether. He contributed humorous cartoons occasionally to Americana.

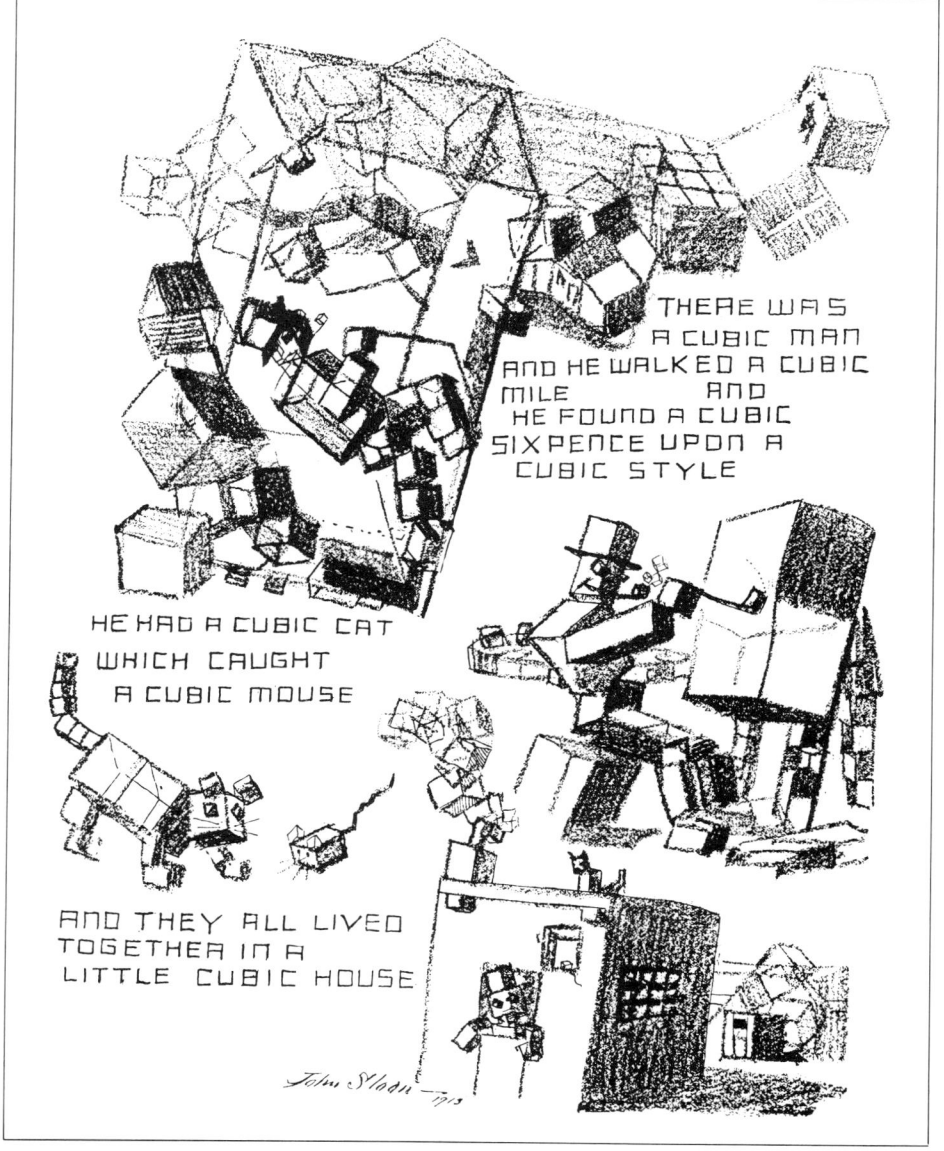

OPPOSITE
Ludlow, Colorado, **The Masses**, June, 1914. Col. Ben Goldstein.

RIGHT
A Slight Attack of Third Dementia, **The Masses**, April, 1913. Private col.

TOP
Benediction in Georgia, **The Masses**, May, 1917. Col. Ben Goldstein. (Original: Lithograph, 1916. 16⅛ x 20. M. 12.)

BOTTOM
Billy Sunday, 1923. Lithograph. 9 x 16⅛. M. 143. Print Room, Boston Public Library.

George Bellows 1882–1925

WHEN HE ARRIVED IN NEW York from Columbus, Ohio, in 1904, Bellows was an athletic, sports-loving extrovert who was soon playing semi-professional baseball in Central Park. Unintellectual, direct, gregarious, he made friends among the group gathered around Robert Henri, his first mentor, and quickly assimilated Henri's philosophy: paint what you see around you. Like his other guide, John Sloan, he prowled the streets of New York, but with less romantic vision, more focus on the sordid and the poor. He painted the streets and the slum kids, the Hudson River, the popular prize fights and, later, numerous landscapes — everything he observed about him. By 1907 he was accepted for the National Academy shows.

Through Sloan's influence, he began contributing to *The Masses* in 1913, often expanding his graphic commentaries into paintings. His ironic "Why Don't They All Go to the Country for a Vacation?," for example, developed into his oil painting "The Cliff Dwellers." Vaguely anarchist, he shared Sloan's distress at poverty and yearned for a more equitable society.

Except for commissioned portraits — often unsuccessful — Bellows usually plunged directly into a subject that appealed to him. His delight in the wonder of life is in his paintings, and his audience appreciated sharing his joy. He helped prepare the Armory Show, but its influence on his painting was nil. He preferred to continue to portray what he considered real in American life.

Bellows despised revivalist preachers especially, and satirized them and their frenzied followers in drawings, prints and paintings. He made a devastating print and painting of the most charismatic of the fundamentalists, Billy Sunday. His reaction to the dynamic preacher reveals much of his social philosophy: "I believe Billy Sunday is the worst thing that happened to America. He is Prussianism personified. His whole purpose is to force authority against beauty. He is against freedom, he wants a religious autocracy, he is such a reactionary that he almost makes me an anarchist."

Bellows's "Benediction in Georgia," drawn for *The Masses* in 1917 and later made into a lithograph, was so effective that it stimulated several stories and articles after it appeared. The hollowness of the Pecksniffian sermon is reflected in the impassive, expressionless faces of the convicts. The parson does not seem to be

Charles E. Albright. Pen and ink. 9⅜ x 7¼. Columbus Museum of Art.

Superior Brains: Business Men's Class, **The Masses**, April, 1913. Beinecke Rare Book Library, Yale University. (Also, lithograph, 1916. 11⅝ x 7⅛. M. 20.)

convincing even himself. The Stygian blackness of the walls, more apparent in the lithograph, enhances the caustic bite of this Brechtian scene.

Bellows's contributions to *The Masses* included the lightly satirical. His "Businessmen's Class" of 1913 reflects the athlete's amused condescension toward the paunchy and the skinny and the radical's disdain for the self-improving bourgeois, making them ludicrous but not depriving them of their humanity. He redrew it as a lithograph.

His satirical bent carried over into caricature, as in this *portrait charge* of Charles E. Albright, classically executed, with exaggerated head and shortened body.

In 1917 he drew a strong anti-war cartoon: Christ in prison stripes, indicted for discouraging enlistment; but by the time it was published, in July, Bellows had completely changed his mind and had become ardently pro-war. His position cut him off from his associates on *The Masses*. During the war he executed a series of anti-German lithographs and he dropped cartooning altogether.

Stuart Davis *1894–1964*

Like John Sloan and George Bellows, Davis was guided by Robert Henri, and like them he obeyed Henri's dictum to explore the streets of New York with sketchbook in hand. But there the similarity ends. What caught Davis's imagination was not the people but the spirit, the symbols, the emblematic images. Long before Pop art, his signs, numbers and calligraphy were integral components of his paintings, together with billboards, gas stations, highway markers, glaring headlines and other paraphernalia of contemporaneity. "I wanted something solid, so I picked out things instead of manners," he said later. His "things" came to include mundane objects — an electric fan, an eggbeater, a rubber glove — which he wove into geometric patterns. Above all, his evenings of listening to the improvisations of jazz and ragtime inspired him to translate the rhythm and the cacophony of the big city into semi-abstract paintings with jazzy, staccato effects of color.

An opinionated battler who plunged into controversy, Davis was politically active for many years. With Sloan as mentor, he inevitably became involved in *The Masses*, contributing more than 30 drawings for the magazine from March, 1913, until April, 1917, when he quit together with Sloan after the controversy over editorial control of the art. His contributions were generous, enthusiastic and sincere, but with inconsistent results. His cartoons often lacked subtlety; occasionally he even had to label his figures to compensate for the ambiguity of their symbolism. His political points were frequently heavy-handed, obvious; his social themes were more effective. His draftsmanship reflected his uncertainty in this medium; it was often labored, lacking in precision and facility of line. He was more at home in illustration with an element of social comment, as in his drawings of prostitutes in the streets, or in fantasies, such as his haunting "New Year's Eve."

Davis's "The Dignity of the Uniform" is a sardonic commentary on the Ludlow Massacre that John Sloan had depicted on the cover of *The Masses* the preceding month. It was charged that the National Guard, which had committed the slaughter at the beck of the mine owners, had recruited professional strike-breakers into its ranks before leaving the state capital for Ludlow. Here they are being outfitted. The perspective ingeniously

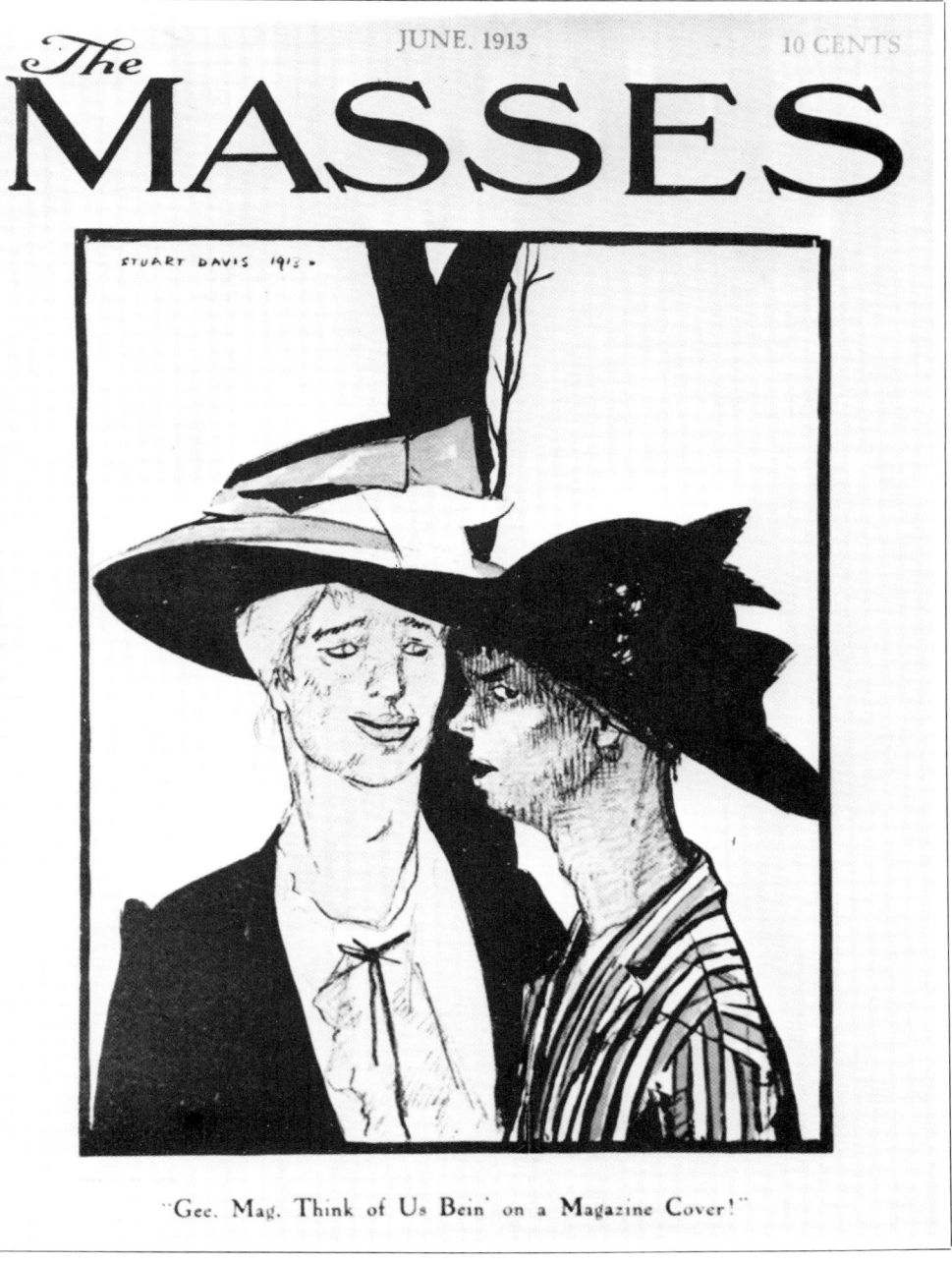

Gee. Mag, **The Masses**, June, 1913. Col. Ben Goldstein. (Original: Pen and ink. 20 x 16. Col. Earl Davis.)

107

ABOVE
May Day, **Art Front**, May, 1935.
Col. Earl Davis.
BELOW
The Dignity of the Uniform, **The Masses**, July, 1914. Col. Ben Goldstein.
OPPOSITE
Restoring the Peon to the Land, **The Masses**, April, 1914. Col. Ben Goldstein.

heightens them and allows a glimpse of their pending armed role. Davis's handling of the figures is convincing; his labeling of the mine owner gives the cartoon a didactic quality that weakens it. He was not an instinctive cartoonist.

"Restoring the Peon to the Land" is Davis's bitter comment on Mexican General Huerta's practice of shooting peasants who had broken up large estates in the mistaken belief that the revolution was at hand. Again Davis displays compassion and political insight, but his draftsmanship is insecure and his composition lacks cohesion.

Davis's "Gee Mag, Think of Us Being on a Magazine Cover" is an amusing if serendipitous satire on the women's magazines whose covers were adorned with portraits of stylish and beautiful society ladies. Davis had drawn his two slum girls for an inside-page cartoon. At an editorial meeting of *The Masses*, John Sloan had the inspiration to make it a cover picture.

During the Depression, the combative Davis was so busy with political action that he had little time for painting. At one time he was both secretary of the American Artists Congress and an editor of *Art Front*, organ of the Artists Union. His May Day cover for *Art Front* marked a considerable advance over most of his representational drawings for *The Masses* of 20 years before. Avoiding the clichés of Social Realism so popular among his colleagues, his collage-like drawing speaks to his artist-audience in its own idiom, leaves the exhortation to slogans in the banners. The touch of Cubism in the tools, the areas of dotting, zigzagging and straight lines, the calligraphy of "Solidarity" are all elements incorporated into his paintings.

Davis could not seem to manage both political involvement and painting. By the Forties he began to concentrate on his painting. In 1945 the Museum of Modern Art gave him a retrospective exhibition. (In his review of the show, Ad Reinhardt regretted that the pugnacious Davis was no longer politically active or involved with artists' groups.)

RESTORING THE PEON TO THE LAND
(As Huerta Does It)

"This is her first lynching."

Reginald Marsh 1898–1954

REGINALD MARSH WAS A YALE graduate who derided his own social class and displayed a sensitive awareness of the less fortunate he observed as he wandered through the streets of New York, sketchbook in hand. Draftsmanship was his lifelong preoccupation. Despite an early scorn for painting ("a laborious way to make a dead drawing"), he eventually turned to canvas, but some of his paintings seem like colored drawings.

From the beginning, Marsh concentrated on line, making free-lance illustrations for *The New York Evening Post, Vanity Fair, Harper's Magazine* and the *New York Herald*. As a staff artist for the *New York Daily News*, he covered trials, night clubs and vaudeville with his sketchbook.

Marsh also created a number of cartoons that reflected a social consciousness rather than any radical political philosophy. His deeply felt sympathy for the victims of society was expressed only rarely, but on those occasions it was highly effective. Although he made a few drawings for the *New Masses*, he was criticized by the Communists for his lack of commitment to "the cause." Lloyd Goodrich quotes him as replying, "Well, what should we do — be ashamed of being what we are — or imitate Orozco, Grosz, African sculpture, and draw endless pictures of gas masks, 'Cossacks,' and caricatures of J. P. Morgan?"

Of the drawings that stand out for their incisive comment, most appeared, surprisingly, in *The New Yorker*, which published one of the most haunting images of the Thirties, Marsh's lynching scene, unforgettable caricature of America's darkest side. Rather than draw the obvious, the lynching itself, he offers a psychological study of the mob spirit. Marsh loved a crowd and a spectacle; here he despises both. The leering, vacuous faces are captured in swift, controlled line, unlike the overblown baroque of many of his paintings. The slobbering mouths and gloating eyes eloquently express his contempt.

Marsh was the social conscience of *The New Yorker*, occasionally making surprisingly didactic graphic comment. "Where men accumulate and wealth decays" was the title of one Depression-inspired drawing of skyscrapers and men, dwarfed, slinking in the shadows.

But most of Marsh's numerous cartoons, which he drew for *The New Yorker* from 1925 to 1944, were gay and frothy, in the tone but not the style of Villon. Some, like Villon's, had a sting as well, making fun of the "upper classes," as in "Long Island Nights." Unlike many *New Yorker* artists, Marsh liked to include telling background detail — in this case, the flimsy dress, the doll on the floor, the pompous portrait.

Whether he drew or painted Bowery bums, burlesque strippers, middle-aged voyeurs, fleshy Coney Island bathers, or doll-faced shopgirls, Marsh displayed a zestful appreciation of his subjects — or commiseration with them.

LONG ISLAND NIGHTS
"Don't you simply adore the peasantry?"

OPPOSITE
This is her first lynching, **The New Yorker**, Sept. 8, 1934. © 1934, 1962, The New Yorker Magazine.

LEFT
Long Island Nights, **The New Yorker**, Dec. 18, 1926. © 1926, 1954, The New Yorker Magazine.

HOW TO LOOK AT MODERN ART IN AMERICA
by Ad Reinhardt

Here's a guide to the galleries—the art world in a nutshell—a tree of contemporary art from pure (abstract) "paintings" (on your left) to pure (illustrative) "pictures" (down on your right). If you know what you like but don't know anything about art, you'll find the artists on the left hardest to understand, and the names on the right easiest and most familiar (famous). You can start in the cornfields, where no demand is made on you and work your way up and around. Be especially careful of those curious schools situated on that overloaded section of the tree, which somehow think of themselves as being both abstract and pictorial (as if they could be both today). The best way to escape from all this is to paint yourself. If you have any friends that we overlooked, here are some extra leaves. Fill in and paste up...

Ad Reinhardt 1913–1967

HIS PURITANICAL STREAK had a strong effect on his politics and on his relations with his colleagues — and perhaps a marginal effect on his paintings. He was politically active all his life, deeply involved in "causes" — civil rights, civil liberties, unions, opposition to the Vietnam War — and his overworked conscience gradually impelled him to become the guardian of the morals of the art world.

But Reinhardt was as much Puck as Savonarola. Although he eventually satirized nearly all his colleagues, competitors, awards, museums, critics and just about every aspect of the contemporary art scene, he did it with such wit, in meticulously executed cartoons and in Joycean verbal fireworks, that for a time most artists pinned up his tirades on the walls of their studios. A few threatened suit — and might have won.

Ironically, the more he was involved in political work, the more his paintings became devoid of any hint of content; the more he verbalized his theories of art and his disdain for the art establishment, the more his paintings eliminated any associative connotation. Thomas B. Hess expressed it well: "As he took more and more out of his art, he put more and more into his satires. It was as if, while painting, he had a thirst for words and images, for immensely complicated iconologies, for direct communication in vulgar jokes, scholarly asides, erudite games of wit, Til Eulenspiegel pranks. As the paintings became more and more spare, the appetite for verbal complications increased. On the other hand, as his satires (and essays, lectures, conversation) became more and more fluent, erudite, poetic, noisy — jumbling shrill voice and pullulating image — he would turn to his paintings for calm and serene contemplation, leaving only the slightest jingle of a hue or a line in their void."

He rigidly compartmentalized his politics and his art, content to believe that "esthetic quality is always socially meaningful," echoing Signac and other anarchist Neo-Impressionists. In his continuous search for "pure," non-associative art, his work gradually evolved from synthetic Cubism through collage and geometric abstraction and color-brick painting to the monochromatic purity of his so-called "black" paintings. The guru of minimal art, his art-as-art theories were the terminal for the nineteenth century's "art-for-art's-sake"

ABOVE
Returned, No Thanks, **New Masses**, Jan. 3, 1939. Private col.

OPPOSITE
How To Look at Modern Art in America, **PM**, June 2, 1946. Col. Seymour Hacker.

115

philosophy. "Art is art-as-art and everything else is everything else," he declared, typically parodying Gertrude Stein while being deadly serious. He was the number one anti-academic of all time, believing that art should never present life or reality or nature or myth or symbols or visions, for these, he felt, were, as in medieval times, for "the minds of the ignorant."

During the Thirties his taste for cartooning found outlet in the radical, Communist-backed *New Masses*, for which he occasionally drew spot drawings or unsubtle political cartoons. In this one, wooden dolls of many of the *bêtes-noires* of the left — J. P. Morgan, Hitler, Mussolini, the appeasing Prime Ministers Chamberlain and Daladier, etc. — are tossed back at Santa Claus's door. Although the style is reminiscent of Stuart Davis, Reinhardt is here already evolving his own signature — Chaplinesque, puppet-like figures, blunt, straight, unadorned lines.

In 1943 he went to work for the liberal New York newspaper *PM*. War service interrupted his work, but in 1946 and 1947 his satirical talents flowered in a popular series of 23 ostensibly instructive cartoons-with-text guides to looking at art. All his life he collected cartoons, details from old engravings, characters from illustrations, line cuts of historical personalities, old photos, as well as quotations and dictionaries and other literary sources for his endless puns and erudite references. From this rich grab bag, he embellished and enriched his art cartoons, to which he added, in the later ones, alliteration, puns, plays on words and names. His culture-hungry *PM* readers eagerly swallowed the series, but few realized that the superficial "How to" guides to modern art were in part parodies of textbooks and other guides to abstract art that greatly oversimplified modern art. And his own prejudices misinformed his audience. He equated realist art, which he despised, with big business and reaction, while he presented abstract art as a populist movement.

His subjects in the *PM* series ran from general instruction ("How to Look at Things Again," "How to Look at Nothing," "How to Look at Iconography," "How to Look at Space," etc.) to the specifics of contemporary art — Abstract, Surrealist, etc. His "How to Look at Low (Surrealist) Art" is typical of his more didactic, somewhat tongue-in-cheek "lessons," illustrated with both his own cartoons and the icons dredged out of his voluminous files. His position was best expressed in the first panel that appeared in most of the series: "Ha Ha What does this represent?" asks the amused spectator. "What do you represent?" replies the abstract painting.

The cartoon that caused the greatest stir (or consternation or amusement or anger) among his fellow-artists was "How

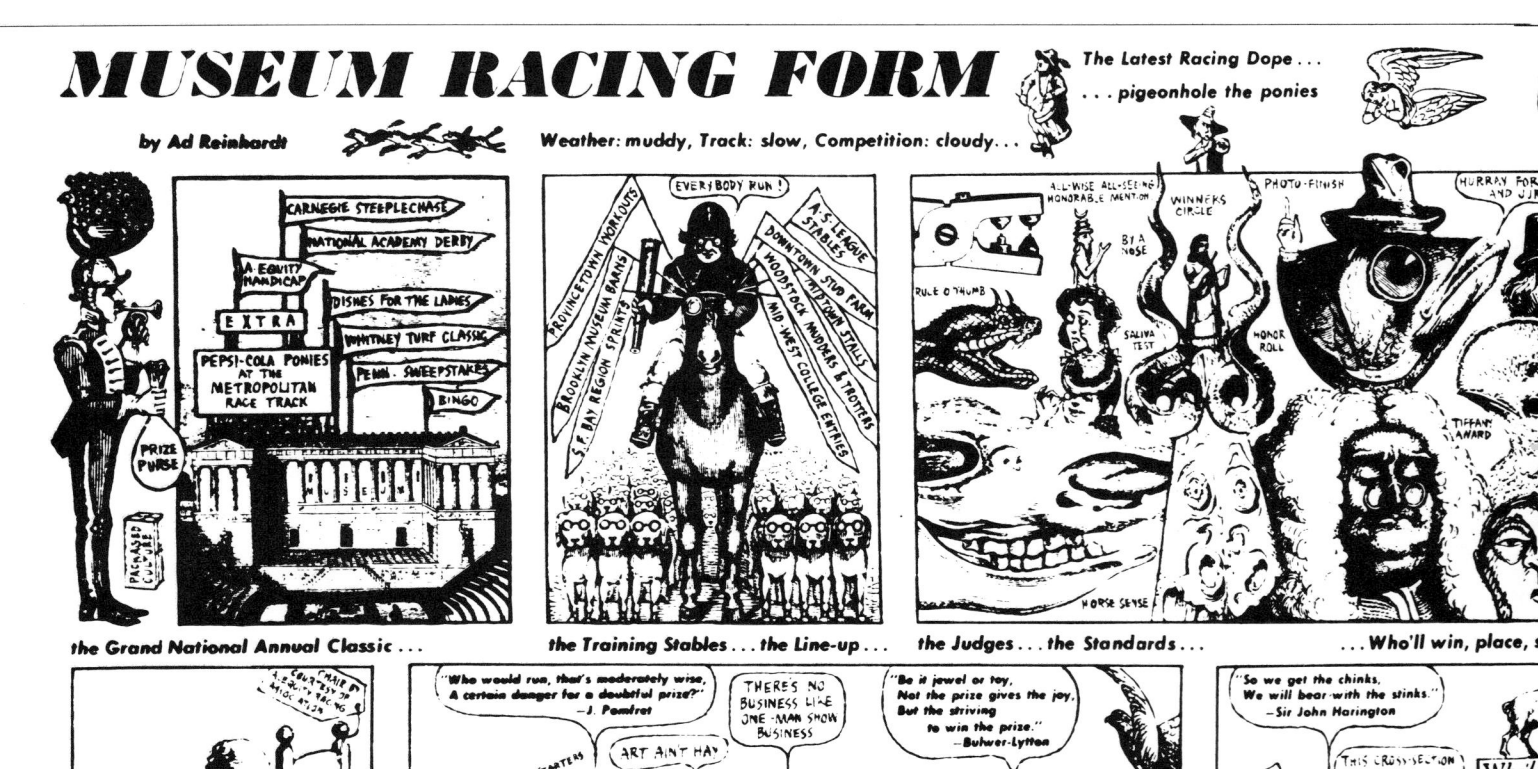

the Hopes...

the Bandwagon...

the Race... cross-country...

to Look at Modern Art in America." His rough division of contemporary artists into various schools, more or less accurate — often less than more — parodied the guide to "isms" by Alfred Barr of the Museum of Modern Art. The entire branch of representational art is about to be broken off from the tree by the weight of Reinhardt's pet peeves — "subject matter"; "Mexican art influence" (Diego Rivera's heroic figures were still influential); illustrative art; Pepsi-Cola and other contests (like the French anarchist artists, he hated all competitions, prizes, awards); links to industry. Relegated to the cornfield are the regionalists and the celebrants of the American scene.

In the Fifties and early Sixties, in a series of three cartoons for *trans/formation* and four for *Art News*, and in lectures and essays, he attacked the "whorish" art world with increasing fervor and sarcasm. Puns flowed freely ("This painting miro-go-round is built on feet of klee"). Pronunciamentos poured forth ("The New York School is a nice place to visit, but I would not like to live there"). He particularly excoriated the museum power-houses, the critics and dealers, and the mutual aggrandizement by artists, dealers and critics.

In a panel in "Museum Racing Form" he also satirizes promotion by critics of their favorite artists — Thomas Craven publicizing Thomas Hart Benton, James Thrall Soby pushing Ben Shahn, Alfred Frankfurter backing Rico Lebrun, etc. "There's No Business Like One-Man Show Business," neighs one of the horses in the art race.

Like Cotton Mather, he thundered that the contemporary scene was a den of corruption (his fellow-artists the sinners). He again categorized "schools" with vitriolic acidity — "Coney Island Trashbasket School," "Great Sweatshop Style," "Mud-Pie School," "I Hear America

BELOW
Museum Racing Forum, **trans/formation**, Nov. 2, 1951. (Original: Drawing. Collage of ink and paper. 8¼ x 21½. Whitney Museum of American Art.)

NEXT PAGE
How To Look at Low (Surrealist) Art, **PM**, March 24, 1946. Col. Seymour Hacker.

the Bookies...the Bets...   the Tip-sheets...   the Professional Racing Association...

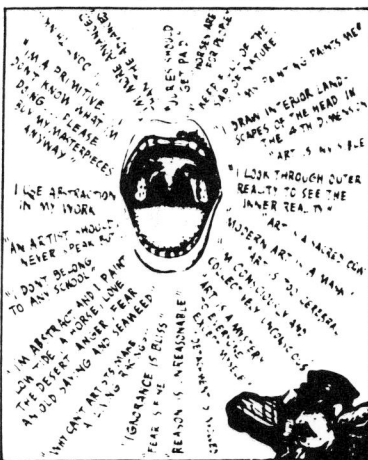

the Racing Results...the Finish...   the Leading Jockeys...the season's Averages...   Out of the Horses' Mouth...

Singing Schools," "Fine Art in Advertising Abstraction," "Buck Rogers (25th Century) Abstraction," and so on.

In "Art of Life of Art," the language became even more Joycean, the images more monstrous, the nightmarish quality perhaps reflecting his own psychoanalysis. "Paint the way the wind blows and get your finger in the pie in the sky," "Hold an inner-fire sale," "Woo a moneybag and let true luck run its course," "Let your monstrous subconscious make a quick buck for yourself." Not surprisingly, Reinhardt's caustic maxims won him few friends. "Founding Fathers Follyday" taunted the strivers and achievers (though, of course, he wanted success himself). His "Portend of the Artist as a Young Mandala" continued the attack but also reflected his own interest in mysticism. He capped the series of seven with an update of his Modern Art tree. By then many of his colleagues were no longer laughing.

118

Bibliography

Adhémar, Jean, "Les journeaux amusants et les premiers peintres cubistes," *L'Oeil*, IV, April 15, 1955.
Alexandre, Arsène, *L'art du rire et de la caricature*, Paris, 1892.
Arts et Métiers Graphiques, No. 31, Sept. 15, 1932, special issue, "Caricatures."
Ashbee, C.R., *Caricature*, London, 1928.

Baudelaire, Charles, *Curiosités esthètiques et autres écrits sur l'art*, Paris, 1968.
— *The mirror of art*, London, 1955.
Bayard, Emile, *La caricature et les caricaturistes*, Paris, 1900.
Bechtel, Edwin deT., *Freedom of the press and l'Association mensuelle. Philipon vs. Louis-Philippe*, New York, 1952.
Bellet, Roger, *Presse et journalisme sous le deuxième Empire*, Paris, 1967.
Blum, André, *La caricature révolutionnaire*, Paris, 1916.
— *L'estampe satirique en France pendant les guerres de réligion*, Paris, 1917.
Brinton, Selwyn, *The eighteenth century in English caricature*, London, 1904.

Carco, Francis, *Les Humoristes*, Paris, 1921.
Chadefeux, Marie-Claude, "Le Salon Caricatural de 1846 et les autres salons caricatureaux," *Gazette des Beaux-Arts*, March, 1968.
Champfleury (Jules-Francois-Félix Fleury), *Histoire de la Caricature*, 5 vols., Paris, 1867–1874.
Coupe, W.A., "The German cartoon and the revolution of 1848," *Comparative Studies in History and Society*, IX, 1967.

Dardel, Aline, *Catalogue des dessins et publications illustrées du journal anarchiste 'Les Temps Nouveaux,' 1895–1914*. Doctoral thesis, University of Paris, 1980.
— "Illustrateurs et satiristes," *Le Gazette de l'Hotel Drouot*, 6 articles, July 10, 1981–Dec. 18, 1981.
Davies, Randall, *Caricature of today*, London, 1928.
Dayot, Armand, *Les maîtres de la caricature française au XIXe siècle*, Paris, 1888.
Deberdt, Raoul, *La caricature et l'humour au XIXe siècle*, Paris, n. d.
Dixmier, Elizabeth and Michel, *L'Assiette au Beurre: revue satirique illustrée*, Paris, 1974.
Dusart, Cornélis, *Les héros de la ligue ou la procession monacle conduitte par Louis XIV pour la conversion de Protestants de son royaume*, Paris, 1691.

Egbert, Donald Drew, *Social radicalism and the arts; western Europe*, New York, 1970.
Everitt, Graham, *English caricaturists and graphic humourists*, London, 1893.

FitzGerald, Richard, *Art and politics: cartoonists of the 'Masses' and 'Liberator,'* Westport, Ct., 1973.
Fuchs, Eduard, *Die karicatur der europaischen volker vom altertum bis zur neuzeit*, Berlin, 1901.
— *Die frau in der karikatur*, Munich, 1906.
— *Der weltkrieg in der karikatur*, Munich, 1916.

Gaultier, Paul, *Le rire et la caricature*, Paris, 1906.
George, M. Dorothy, *English political caricature: a study of opinion and propaganda*, London, 2 vols., 1959.
— *Social change and graphic satire, from Hogarth to Cruikshank*, London, 1967.
Getlein, Frank and Dorothy, *The bite of the print*, New York, 1963.
Goldwater, Walter, *Radical periodicals in America, 1890–1950*, New Haven, 1969.
Gombrich, E.H., "The cartoonist's armoury," in *Meditations on a hobby horse*, London, 1963.
— *Art and illusion*, London, 1959.
— and Kris, E., *Caricature*, Harmondsworth, 1940.
Gould, Ann, ed., *Masters of Caricature*, New York, 1981. Introduction and commentary by William Feaver.
Grand-Carteret, John, *Les moeurs et les caricatures en France*, Paris, 1888.

Hahn, O., "Paris: art and anti-art," *Arts*, vol. 41, Summer, 1967.
Herbert, Eugenia W., *The artist and social reform: France and Belgium, 1885–1898*, New Haven, 1961.
Hess, Stephen and Kaplan, Milton, *The ungentlemanly art — a history of American political cartoons*, New York, 1968.
Hill, Draper, *Mr. Gillray, the caricaturist*, London, 1965.
Hillier, Bevis, *Cartoons and caricatures*, London, 1970.
Hofmann, Werner, *Caricature*, New York, 1957.
Hollweck, Ludwig, *Karikaturen von den Fliegenden Blätter bis zum Simplicissimus, 1844–1914*, Munich, 1943.
Holme, Geoffrey, *Caricature of today*, London, 1928.

Kahn, Gustave, *La femme dans la caricature française*, Paris, 1907.
— *Europas fursten im sittenspiegel der karikatur*, Berlin, 1909.
Klingender, F.D., *Hogarth and English caricature*, London, 1944.
— *Art and the Industrial Revolution*, London, 1947.
Kozloff, Max, "Caricatures of Giambattista Tiepolo," *Marsyas*, v. 10, 1960–'61.
Kunzle, David, *The early comic strip*, Berkeley, 1973.

Lambert, Giselle, *Les illustrateurs de l'Assiette au Beurre*, doctoral thesis, Ecole du Louvre, Bibliothèque Nationale, Paris.
Lavater, J.C., *Essay on physiognomy for the promotion of the knowledge and the love of mankind*, London, 1789.
Le Brun, *La physionomie humaine comparée à la physionomie des animaux, d'après les dessins de Le Brun*, Paris, 1927.
Lethève, Jacques, *La caricature et la presse sous la IIIe République*, Paris, 1961.
Lucie-Smith, Edward, *The art of caricature*, Ithaca, 1981.
Lynch, Bohun, *A history of caricature*, London, 1926.

Maeterlinck, L., *Le genre satirique dans la peinture flamande*, Brussels, 1907.
Mahon, Denis, *Studies in seicento art and theory*, London, 1947.
Matthews, Roy T. and Mellini, Peter, *In 'Vanity Fair,'* London and Berkeley, 1982.
Maurice, Arthur B., *The history of the nineteenth century in caricature*, New York, 1904.
Mayor, A. Hyatt, "Renaissance pamphleteers — Savonarola and Luther," *Metropolitan Museum of Art Bulletin*, Oct., 1947.
Melot, Michel, *L'œil qui rit; le pouvoir comique des images*, Fribourg, 1975.

Morin, Louis, *Le dessin humoristique*, Paris, 1913.
Murrell, William, *A history of American graphic humor, 1865–1938*, New York, 1938.

O'Neill, William L., ed., *Echoes of revolt: 'The Masses,' 1911–1917*, Chicago, 1966.

Parton, James, *Caricature and other comic art in all times and in all places*, New York, 1877.
Philippe, Robert, *Political graphics: art as a weapon*, New York, 1981.
Price, Aimée Brown, "Official artists and not-so-official art: covert caricaturists in nineteenth-century France," *Art Journal*, Winter, 1984.

Ragon, Michel, *Le dessin d'humour; histoire de la caricature et du dessin humouristique en France*, Paris, 1960.
— *Les maîtres du dessin satirique*, Paris, 1972.
Revel, J.F., "L'invention de la caricature," *L'Oeil*, no. 109, Jan., 1964.
Robert-Jones, Philippe, "La presse satirique illustrée entre 1860 et 1890," *Etudes de Presse*, VIII, no. 14, 1956.
— *De Daumier à Lautrec*, Paris, 1960.
Roth, Eugen, *Simplicissimus: ein ruckbluck auf die satirische zeitschrift*, Hanover, 1954.

Savory, Jerold J., et al, *The 'Vanity Fair' gallery: a collector's guide to the caricatures*, So. Brunswick, N.J., 1979.
Searle, Ronald, Roy, Claude, and Bornemann, Bernd, *La caricature, art et manifeste*, Geneva, 1974.
Shapiro, Theda, *Painters and politics: the European avant-garde and society, 1900–1925*, New York, 1976.
Shikes, Ralph E., *The indignant eye: the artist as social critic in prints and drawings from the fifteenth century to Picasso*, Boston, 1969.
Spielman, *The history of 'Punch,'* London, 1895.
Stephens, F.D. and George, M. Dorothy, *British Museum catalogue of political and personal satires*, 12 vols., 1978.

Veth, C.A., *Geschiedenis van der Netherlandsche caricatuur*, Leyden, 1921.
— *Die politicke prent in Netherland*, Leyden, 1920.

Warnod, André, *Ceux de la Butte*, Paris, 1947.
Wechsler, Judith, *A human comedy: physiognomy and caricature in 19th century Paris*, Chicago, 1982.
Wright, Thomas, *A history of caricature and grotesque in literature and art*, London, 1875.

Catalogues

Cartoon and caricature from Hogarth to Hoffnung, Arts Council of Great Britain, London, 1962. Foreword by Osbert Lancaster. Introduction by Draper Hill.
Arte e resistenza in Europe, Bologna, 1965. Preface by Jean Cassou.
Engagierte kunst, Gesellschaftskritische grafik seit Goya, Vienna, 1966. Introduction by Ulrich Maumgartner.
Le dessin d'humour du XVe siecle à nos jours, Bibliothèque Nationale, Paris, 1971. Comment by Michel Melot.
Caricature and its role in graphic satire, Rhode Island School of Design and Brown University, Providence, 1971.
The cult of images, University of California, Santa Barbara, 1977. Introduction by Beatrice Farwell.

Simplicissimus: The art of Germany's most influential satire magazine (1866–1944), Goethe House and La Boetie, New York, 1979. Text by Mark Rosenthal, edited by Steven Heller.
The comic art show: cartoons in painting and popular culture, Whitney Museum of American Art, New York, 1983. Introduction by John Carlin and Sheena Wagstaff.

Bibliographies of the painters and sources of quotations

These bibliographies list only those works most germane to the painter as caricaturist.

Delacroix

Delteil, Loys, *Le peintre-graveur illustré*, Paris, 1906–30.
Robeaut, Alfred, *L'oeuvre complèt d'Eugène Delacroix*, New York, 1969, rep. ed. Commentary by Ernest Chesneau.
Baudelaire, Charles, "The life and work of Eugène Delacroix," rep. in *The Painter of modern life and other essays*, tr. by Jonathan Mayne, London, 1964.
Alexandre, Arsène, *L'art du rire et du caricature*, op. cit.
Florisoone, Michel, "Comment Delacroix a-t-il connu les 'Caprices' de Goya?" *Bulletin de la Société de l'Histoire de l'Art Francais*, année 1957, pp. 131–144.
Grand-Carteret, John, *Les moeurs et las caricatures en France*, op. cit.

Puvis de Chavannes

Les caricatures de Puvis de Chavannes, Paris, 1906, Preface by Marcelle Adam.
Alexandre, Arsène, *Puvis de Chavannes*, London and New York, 1905.
Price, Aimée Brown, "Official artists and not-so-official art: covert caricatures in nineteenth-century France," op. cit.

Pissarro

Turpitudes Sociales, facsimile ed., Geneva, 1972, with separate essay by André Fermiger, "Pissarro et l'anarchisme."
Brettell, Richard and Lloyd, Christopher, *A catalogue of the drawings by Camille Pissarro in the Ashmolean Museum, Oxford*, Oxford, 1980.
Shikes, Ralph E. and Harper, Paula, *Pissarro: his life and work*, New York, 1980.
"You feel in his drawings . . ." Rewald, John, ed., *Camille Pissarro: Letters to his son Lucien*, op. cit., Feb. 17, 1884.
"Rather incline . . ." ibid., July 5, 1883.
"Fortunately, I had done . . ." ibid., Sept. 30, 1892.
Pissarro, Arts Council of Great Britain and the Museum of Fine Arts, Boston, 1980.

Manet

Guérin, Marcel, *L'oeuvre gravé de Manet*, Paris, 1944.
Harris, Jean C., *Edouard Manet: graphic works*, New York, 1970.
Moreau-Nélaton, Etienne, *Manet raconté par lui-meme*, Paris, 1926.
Guiffrey, Jean, ed., *Lettres illustrées d'Edouard Manet*, Paris, n.d.
"All the officers . . ." Moreau-Nélaton, p. 14.

Monet

Wildenstein, Daniel, *Monet*, Milan, 1971, pp. 84–93.
Rouart, Denis, *Claude Monet*, New York, 1958.

Edwards, Hugh, "The caricatures of Claude Monet," *Bulletin of the Art Institute of Chicago*, Sept.–Oct., 1943, vol. 37, no. 5.
Walter, Rodolphe, "Claude Monet as caricaturist: a clandestine apprenticeship," *Apollo*, June, 1976, vol. 103.
Roberts-Jones, Philippe, *La caricature du 2ème Empire*, op. cit.
"I used to burst . . ." Rouart, *Claude Monet*, op. cit., p. 22.

Gauguin

Danielsson, Bengt, *Gauguin in the south seas*, New York, 1966.
Danielsson and Patrick O'Reilly, *Gauguin, journaliste à Tahiti et ses articles des 'Guêpes,'* Paris 1966.
Andersen, Wayne (with the assistance of Barbara Klein), *Gauguin's Paradise Lost*, New York, 1971.
Guérin, Marcel, *L'oeuvre gravé de Paul Gauguin*, Paris, 1927.
Pickvance, Ronald, *The drawings of Gauguin*, London, 1970.
Onze menus de Paul Gauguin, Geneva, 1950. Introduction by Robert Rey.
Le Sourire de Paul Gauguin, facsimile ed., Paris, 1952. Introduction by L.-J. Bouge.
"That's how I became . . ." Gauguin, *Avant et Après*, quoted in Danielsson and O'Reilly, p. 7.
"He's always on the side . . ." Rewald, *Pissarro: Letters to his son Lucien*, op. cit. Nov. 20, 1883.

Forain

Bory, Jean-Francois, *Forain*, Paris, 1979.
Browse, Lillian, *Forain, the painter*, London, 1978.
Guérin, Marcel, *J.L. Forain, lithographe*, Paris, 1910.
Magne, Jacqueline, *Forain, témoin de son temps*, Marseille, 1973.
Alexandre, Arsène, *L'art du rire et caricature*, op cit.
Gaultier, Paul, *Le rire et la caricature*, op. cit.
Jean-Louis Forain, Artist, realist, humanist, International Exhibitions Foundation, Washington, D.C., 1982. Preface by Yves Brayer, catalogue by Alicia Faxon.
"Ce Forain a une langue . . ." Goncourt Journal, March 25, 1882, quoted in Browse, op. cit., p. 10.
"what a bourgeois soul . . ." quoted in *The indignant eye*, op. cit., p. 232.

Luce

Hommes d'Aujourd'hui, July, 1890.
Cazeau, Philippe, *Maximilien Luce*, Lausanne, Paris, 1982.
Sutter, Jean, *Luce: les traveaux et les jours*, Geneva, n.d.
Tabarant, A. *Maximilien Luce*, Paris, 1928.
Maximilien Luce, Palais des Beaux-Arts, Charleroi, Belgium, 1966.
Alexandre, Arsène, "Maximilien Luce," *Cahiers de Belgique*, Dec., 1929.
Dardel, Aline, "Illustrateurs et satiristes: V- La revolte ou le drapeau noir: Luce, Camille et Lucien Pissarro," *Gazette de l'Hotel Drouot*, Dec. 11, 1981, no. 44.
"Luce is everywhere . . ." Letter from Lucien Pissarro to Camille Pissarro, April 6, 1896, Ashmolean Museum, Oxford.

Anquetin

Bernard, Emile, *Anquetin*, Paris, 1932.
Welsh-Ovsharov, Bogomila, *Vincent van Gogh and the birth of Cloisonism*, Toronto Museum of Art, 1981.
Sherard, Robert H. "Louis Anquetin, painter," *Art Journal*, London, new series, 1899, pp. 85–90.

"Toulouse-Lautrec and Anquetin . . ." Sir William Rothenstein, *Men and Memories*, London, 1931, p. 63.
"There is only one . . ." Sherard, op. cit., p. 87.
"Another who rummages . . ." *Camille Pissarro: letters to his son Lucien*, op. cit., March 23, 1898.

Signac

Besson, George, *Paul Signac*, Paris, 1950.
Cachin, Françoise, *Paul Signac*, Greenwich, Ct., 1971. Translated by Michael Bullock.
Kornfeld, E. W. and Wick, P. A., *Catalogue raisonné de l'oeuvre gravé de Paul Signac*, Berne, 1974.
Herbert, Eugenia W., *The artist and social reform*, op. cit.
Paul Signac, Museé du Louvre, 1963, catalogue by Marie Thérèse Lemoyne de Forges.
John Rewald, "Extraits du journal inédit de Paul Signac, *Gazette des Beaux-Arts*, 6th series, vol. 36, July–Sept., 1949, pp. 97–128; vol. 39, 1952, pp. 265–284; vol. 42, 1953, pp. 27–57.
Herbert, Robert L. and Herbert, Eugenia W., "Artists and anarchism: unpublished letters of Pissarro, Signac and others," *Burlington Magazine*, vol. 102, Nov. and Dec., 1960.
"The anarchist painter . . ." *La Révolte*, June 13–19, unsigned but attributed to Signac.
"Nourished by your principles . . ." Aug. 1, 1916, quoted in Herbert and Herbert, op. cit., Dec., 1960, p. 520.

Toulouse-Lautrec

Huisman, P. and Dortu, M. G., *Lautrec by Lautrec*, New York, 1964.
Joyant, Maurice, *Henri de Toulouse-Lautrec*, Paris, 1926.
Adhémar, Jean, *Toulouse-Lautrec; his complete lithographs and drypoints*, New York, 1965.
Dortu, M. G., *Toulouse-Lautrec et son oeuvre*, 7 vols.
Roberts-Jones, Philippe, *La Caricature du 2ème Empire*, op. cit.
Prints and drawings from the collection of Mr. and Mrs. Sherman Butler, Stanford, 1971. Introduction by Lorenz Eitner.
"He was perhaps . . ." Eitner, op. cit., p. 5.

Vallotton

Hahnloser-Buhler, Hedy, *Félix Vallotton et ses amis*, Paris, 1936.
— *Félix Vallotton, 1865–1928*, Zurich, 1927–28, 2 vols., vol. 1, *Der graphiker*.
Godefroy, Louis, *L'oeuvre gravé de Félix Vallotton*, Paris, 1932.
Vallotton, Maxime and Goerg, Charles, *Félix Vallotton: Catalogue raisonné de l'oeuvre gravé et lithographié*, Geneva, 1972.
The graphic work of Félix Vallotton and the Nabis, Kovler Gallery, Chicago, 1970.
Prints and drawings of Félix Vallotton, Smithsonian Institution, Washington, 1971.
The graphic work of Félix Vallotton, Great Britain Arts Council, London, 1976.
Dardel, Aline, "Illustrateurs et satiristes," *Le Gazette de l'Hotel Drouot*, no. 38, Oct. 30, 1981.
Félix Vallotton, Hirschl and Adler Gallery, New York, 1970.

Kupka

Vachtlova, Ludmila, *Frank Kupka, pioneer of abstract art*, New York, 1968. Tr. by Z. Lederer.
Letters to Jean Grave, Institut Francais d'Histoire Sociale.

Adhémar, Jean, "Les journeaux amusants", *op. cit.*
Kupka, Musée d'Art Moderne, Paris, 1958.
Frantisek Kupka: a retrospective, 1871–1957, Guggenheim Museum, 1975. Preface by Thomas M. Messer.

Villon

Mellquist, Jerome, *Les caricatures de Jacques Villon et le marge de l'indulgence*, Geneva, 1960. Tr. from English by Berthe Vielliemin.
Ginestat, Colette and Pouillon, Catherine, *Jacques Villon – Les estampes et les illustrations – Catalogue raisonné*, Paris, c. 1979.
Lieberman, W. S., *Jacques Villon: his graphic art*, New York, 1953.
Jacques Villon: master printmaker, R.M. Light & Co., New York, 1964. Introduction by Francis Steegmuller.
Jacques Villon, master of graphic art, 1875–1963, Museum of Fine Arts, Boston, 1966. Preface by Jean Cassou.
Jacques Villon, Fogg Art Museum, Cambridge, Mass., 1976. Edited by Daniel Robbins.
Campbell, Lawrence, "The father of modern printmaking," *Art News*, v. 66, no. 8, Dec., 1967.
"offers many opportunities . . ." Steegmuller, *op. cit.*, p. 5.
"he acquired a rare . . ." Ginestat and Pouillon, *op. cit.*, p. 451.

van Dongen

Chaumeil, Louis, *Van Dongen*, Paris, 1967.
Wentinek, Charles, *Van Dongen*, Amsterdam, n. d.
Giry, Marcel, *Fauvism: origins and development*, New York, 1982.
Lambert, Giselle, *Les illustrateurs de l'Assiette au Beurre*, op. cit.
"Bums, madmen, masters," unsigned, *Life*, Feb. 8, 1960, vol. 8, no. 5, pp. 91–94.
"The things I wanted . . ." Wentinek, *op. cit.*, p. 8.
"Most of us still had . . ." *Life*, *op. cit.*, p. 94.

Marcoussis

La Franchis, Jean, *Marcoussis, sa vie, son oeuvre*, Paris, 1961.
Louis Marcoussis, Musée National d'Art Modern, Paris, 1964. Preface by Jean Cassou, catalogue by Antoinette Hure.
Marcoussis: l'ami des poètes, Bibliothèque Nationale, Paris, 1972. Introduction by Jean Adhémar, catalogue by Anne-Marie Mousseique de Leyritz.

Picasso

Zervos, Christian, *Pablo Picasso*, 30 vols., Paris, 1932–1975.
A suite of 180 drawings by Picasso, Nov. 28, 1953–Feb. 3, 1954, New York, 1954. Preface by Teriade, "Picasso and the human comedy," by Michel Leiris.
Blunt, Anthony and Pool, Phoebe, *Picasso: the formative years*, New York, 1962.
Palau i Fabre, Josep, *Picasso, the early years*, 1881–1907, New York, 1981.
Barr, Alfred H. Jr., *Picasso: fifty years of his art*, New York, rep. ed., 1966.
Penrose, Roland, *Picasso — his life and work*, New York, 1959.
El Quatre Gats: art in Barcelona around 1900, Princeton University, 1978. Catalogue by Marilyn McCully.
Pablo Picasso, Museum of Modern Art, New York, 1980. Edited by William Rubin, chronology by Jane Fluegel.
"this was not so stupid . . ." Penrose, *op. cit.*, p. 126.
Tr. of "Dream and Lie of Franco," Barr, *op. cit.*, p. 196.

Gris

Gaya-Nuno, Juan Antonio, *Juan Gris*, Boston, 1975.
Kahnweiler, D.H., *Juan Gris: his life and work*, London, 1947. Tr. by Douglas Cooper.
Juan Gris, Museum of Modern Art, New York, 1958. Introduction by James Thrall Soby.
Adhémar, Jean, "Les journeaux amusants," *op. cit.*

Landseer

Lennie, Campbell, *Landseer: the Victorian paragon*, London, 1976.
Sir Edwin Landseer, Tate Gallery, London and Philadelphia Museum of Art, 1982. Text by Richard Ormond.
"Landseer gives his . . ." quoted in Weisberg, Gabriel P., "Sir Edwin Landseer: Called by the Wild," *Art News*, March, 1982, p. 122.

Rossetti

Nicoll, John, *Dante Gabriel Rossetti*, New York, 1975.
Waugh, Evelyn, *D.G. Rossetti, his life and work*, London, 1928.
Surtees, Virginia, *Dante Gabriel Rossetti — the paintings and drawings: a catalogue raisonné*, Oxford, 1971.
Rossetti, William Michael, *Some reminiscences*, London, 1906.
Gaunt, William, *The Pre-Raphaelite tragedy*, London, 1942.

Millais

Millais, John G., *The life and letters of Sir John Everett Millais*, 2 vols., London, 1899.
Luytens, Mary, *Millais and the Ruskins*, London, 1967.
Gaunt, William, *The Pre-Raphaelite tragedy*, op. cit.

Burne-Jones

Fitzgerald, Penelope, *Edward Burne-Jones, a biography*, London, 1975.
Bell, Quentin, *Victorian artists*, Cambridge, Mass., 1967.
Lambourne, Lionel, "Paradox and significance of Burne-Jones's caricatures," *Apollo*, Nov., 1975. (Entire issue devoted to Burne-Jones.)
Burne-Jones, the paintings, graphics, decorative work, Arts Council of Great Britain, London, 1973. Introduction by John Christian.
"imagined a world . . ." Bell, *Victorian artists*, *op. cit.*, p. 68.

Tissot

Laver, James *'Vulgar Society,' the romantic career of James Tissot*, London, 1936.
Matthews, Roy T. and Mellini, Peter, *In 'Vanity Fair,'* op. cit.
Savory, Jerrold J. et al, *The 'Vanity Fair' gallery, a collector's guide*, op. cit.

Crane

Crane, Walter, *Cartoons for the cause*, London, 1907, rep. ed.
— *An artist's reminiscences*, London 1907.
Spencer, Isobel, *Walter Crane*, London, 1975.
"my chief hope lies . . ." Spencer, *Walter Crane, op. cit.*, p. 155.

Sickert

Sickert, Walter, *A free house! Or, the artist as craftsman*. Ed. by Osbert Sitwell, London, 1947.
Baron, Wendy, *Sickert*, New York and London, 1973.

Browse, Lillian, *Sickert*, London, 1960.
Sickert, ed. by Lillian Browse, with essay by R.H. Wilenski, London, 1943.
Emmons, Robert, *The life and opinions of Walter Richard Sickert*, London, 1942.
Sutton, Denys, *Walter Sickert, a biography*, London, 1976.
White, Gabriel, "Sickert drawings," *Image*, vol. 7, 1952, pp. 4–47.

Feininger

Prasse, Leona E., *Lyonel Feininger; a definitive catalogue of his graphic work — etchings, lithographs and woodcuts*, Cleveland, 1972.
Scheyer, Ernst, *Lyonel Feininger: caricature and fantasy*, Detroit, 1964.
Feininger/Hartley, Museum of Modern Art, New York, 1944. Essays by Alois J. Schardt and Alfred H. Barr, Jr.
Jacques Villon/Feininger, Institute of Contemporary Art, Boston, 1949. Essay by Frederick S. Wright.
Lyonel Feininger, the formative years, Detroit Institute of Arts, 1964. Introduction by Ernst Scheyer.
Lyonel Feninger: Karikaturen, comic strips, illustrationem, 1888–1915, Museum für Kunst und Gewerbe, Hamburg, 1981. Essays by Ulrich Luckhardt, Martin Sonnabend and Regine Timm.

Pascin

Brodzky, Horace, *Pascin*, London, 1946.
Morand, Paul, *Pascin*, Paris, 1931.
Warnod, Andre, *Pascin*, Paris, 1936. (L'Art d'Aujourd'hui, no. 10)
Drawings by Pascin, Paris, 1967. Introduction by Florent Fels.
P. Cabanne, *Outlaws of art*, London, 1963. Tr. by Denis George.
Pascin, University of California, Berkeley, 1966. Catalogue by Tom L. Freudenheim.
Pascin, Musée d'Art et d'Historique Geneva, 1970. Preface by Gaston Diehl.

Grosz

Grosz, George, *A little yes and a big no: The autobiography of George Grosz*. New York, 1946. Translated by Nola Sachs Dorin.
Baur, John I. H., *George Grosz*, New York, 1954.
Lewis, Beth Irwin, *George Grosz: art and politics in the Weimar Republic*, Madison, Wisc., 1971.
Schneede Uwe, *George Grosz: his life and work*, New York, 1979.
Der Malik Verlag 1916–1917, Ausstellungskatalog, Deutsche Akademe Der Kunst Zu Berlin.

Sloan

Sloan, John, *Gist of art*, New York, 1939.
Brooks, Van Wyck, *John Sloan, a painter's life*, New York, 1955.
DuBois, Guy Pène, *John Sloan*, New York, 1931.
St. John, Bruce, *John Sloan*, New York, 1971.
Fitzgerald, Richard, *Art & politics*, op. cit., pp. 121–161.

Bellows

Braider, Donald, *George Bellows and the Ashcan school of painting*, New York, 1971.
Morgan, C.H., *George Bellows, painter of America*, New York, 1965.
George W. Bellows: his lithographs, New York, 1927. Edited by Emma S. Bellows.
Mason, Lauris, *The lithographs of George Bellows*, Millwood, N.Y., c. 1977.
George Bellows, paintings, drawings and prints, Art Institute of Chicago, 1946. Essays by Eugene Speicher, F.A. Sweet, Carl O. Schniewind.

Davis

Blesh, Rudi, *Stuart Davis*, New York, 1960.
Goosens, Eugene C., *Stuart Davis*, New York, 1959.
Stuart Davis (American Artists Group Monograph no. 6), New York, 1945.
Stuart Davis, Museum of Modern Art, 1945. Essay by James Johnson Sweeney.
Stuart Davis, Walker Art Center, Minneapolis, 1957. Introduction by H.H. Arnason.

Marsh

Goodrich, Lloyd, *Reginald Marsh*, New York, 1972.
Sasowsky, N., *The prints of Reginald Marsh*, New York, 1976.
Reginald Marsh, Whitney Museum of American Art, New York, 1955. Introduction by Lloyd Goodrich.

Shahn

Shahn, Bernarda Bryson, *Ben Shahn*, New York, 1972.
Morse, John D., ed., *Ben Shahn*, New York, 1972.
Soby, James Thrall, *Ben Shahn, his graphic art*, New York, 1957.
Prescott, Kenneth W., *The complete graphic works of Ben Shahn*, New York, 1973.
Ben Shahn; retrospective exhibition, Museum of Modern Art, New York, 1947–1948.
The collected prints of Ben Shahn, Philadelphia Museum of Art, Philadelphia, 1967. Essay by Kneeland McNulty.
Ben Shahn, New Jersey State Museum, Trenton, 1969.
"people who draw. . ." Prescott, *op. cit.*, p. xvi.

Reinhardt

Hess, Thomas B., ed. *The art comics and satire of Ad Reinhardt*, Dusseldorf, Rome, 1973. Facsimiles of 23.
Ad Reinhardt: art comics and satires, Truman Gallery, New York, 1976. Facsimile reproductions. Text by Peter Schjeldahl.
Lippard, Lucy R. *Ad Reinhardt*, New York, 1981.
Kramer, Hilton, "Ad Reinhardt's black humor," *New York Times*, Nov. 27, 1966.
— "Satirizing the art world," *ibid.*, Oct. 17, 1976.
Kozloff, Max, "Andy Warhol and Ad Reinhardt," *Studio International*, Nov., 1971.
"As he took . . ." Hess, *op. cit.*, p. 24.
"art is art-as-art . . ." quoted in *Ad Reinhardt: painting*, The Jewish Museum, New York, essay by Lucy R. Lippard, p. 10.

Index

PAGE NUMBERS IN *ITALICS* REFER TO MAIN DISCUSSIONS OF ARTISTS.

Die Aktion, 97
Americana, 100, 102
Angrand, Charles, 12
Anquetin, Louis, *40–41*
Apollinaire, Guillaume, 62
L'Argent, 53
Art Front, 108, 113
Art News, 117
L'Assiette au Beurre, 12, 13, 50, 53, 58, 59, 61, 69, 70, 85

Bacon, Peggy, 14
Barlach, Ernst, 14
Beardsley, Aubrey, 12, 69
Beckmann, Max, 14
Bellows, George, 9, 13, *104–106*
Berliner Tageblätt, 89, 97
Bernard, Emile, 40
Bernini, G. L., 9
Der Bildermann, 14
Black and White, 83
Blanco y Negro, 69
Der blutige Ernst, 98
Boilly, Louis-Léopold, 11
Bonnard, Pierre, 49
Botticelli, Sandro, 83
Boudin, Eugène, 29
Bracquemond, Felix, 14
Braque, Georges, 62
Brown, Ford Madox, 11
Burne-Jones, Sir Edward, 13, 74, *78–79*, 83
Busch, Wilhelm, 10, 12

Le Canard sauvage, 49, 53
Caran d'Ache, 36, 38
La Caricature, 11
Carracci, Agostino, 9
Carracci, Annibale, 9, 13
Carrière, Eugène, 63
Cassatt, Mary, 14
Cassinelli, Henri, 30
Cézanne, Paul, 35
Le Chambard socialiste, 12, 37, 38
Chap-Book, 49
Le Charivari, 11, 13, 24, 69
Le Chat Noir, 55
Chéret, Jules, 12
Chicago Sunday Tribune, 90
Chirico, Giorgio de, 13
Clarion, 83
Cocorico, 22, 41, 53, 54, 55
Commonweal, 83
Comrade, 85
Corinth, Lovis, 14
Le Courrier Français, 12, 35, 45, 49, 55
Couture, Thomas, 13
Crane, Walter, 9, *82–85*
Le Cri de Paris, 69
Cross, Henri-Edmond, 12, 13, 43

Daumier, Honoré, 8, 10, 11, 12, 14, 24, 35, 50, 58, 97, 101, 102
Davis, Stuart, 13, *107–109*, 116
Decamps, Alexandre, 13
Degas, Edgar, 35, 36, 45, 87
de Kooning, Willem, 13
Delacroix, Eugène, 8, 9, 14, *17–19*
Le Diogène, 27, 30
Dix, Otto, 14
Doré, Paul, 13
Dunoyer de Segonzac, André, 13
Dusart, Cornélis, 9

L'Echo de Paris, 35
En Dehors, 37, 40
Ensor, James, 14
L'Escarmouche, 45, 49
L'Estampe Originale, 49

Feininger, Lyonel, 8, 9, 12, 15, *88–93*, 97
La Feuille, 37, 41
Le Fifre, 36
Le Figaro, 35, 36
Fildes, Luke, 11
Fliegende Blätter, 12, 87
Forain, Jean-Louis, 9, 12, *34–36*, 38, 101
Francesca, Piero della, 21
Frou-Frou, 53, 55, 58

Gauguin, Paul, 8, 13, 21, *31–33*, 35, 63
Der Gegner, 98
Gérôme, Jean, 13
Gil Blas, 35, 55
Gillray, James, 9, 13, 17
Gist of Art, 102
Gonzales, Eva, 14
Gottlob, Fernand, 13
Goya y Lucientes, Francisco José de, 14, 17, 58, 97
Gris, Juan, 9, 11, 55, 62, *68–71*
Grooms, Red, 13
Gropper, William, 13
Grosz, George, 8, 9, 13, 15, *96–100*
Les Guêpes, *31–32*
Guercino, 9
Le Guerre sociale, 37
Guillaume, Albert, 13
Gulbransson, Olaf, 13
Guston, Philip, 13

Harper's Magazine, 111
Heckel, Erich, 14
Heine, T. T., 13
Henri, Robert, 105, 107
Hermann-Paul, René-Georges, 13
Hogarth, William, 10
Holbein, Hans, 9, 13
Homer, Winslow, 13

L'Illustration, 12
L'Imagier, 14
l'Indiscrêt, 58

Jacque, Charles, 13
Le Journal, 61
Judge, 69
Jugend, 49, 94
Justice, 83, 85

Keene, Charles, 11, 24, 87, 101
Keppler, Joseph, 13
Kirchner, Ernst, 14
Klee, Paul, 14
Kokoschka, Oskar, 14
Kollwitz, Käthe, 13
Kubin, Alfred, 12, 13, 97
Kupka, Franz, 8, 9, 11, 25, *52–54*, 55, 56

Landseer, Sir Edwin, 13, *72–73*
Lavater, J. C., 11
Léandre, Charles, 13
Le Brun, Charles, 11
Liberator, 13
Lichtenstein, Roy, 13
Life, 13, 69
Luce, Maximilien, 11, *37–39*, 43, 58
Luks, George, 13
Lustige Blätter, 89, 90

Madrid Cómico, 69
Manet, Edouard, 8, 13, *26–27*, 63
Marc, Franz, 14
Marcoussis, Louis, 8, 11, *60–62*
Marsh, Reginald, 8, 9, 13, *110–111*
Masses, 13, 50, 101, 102, 106, 107, 108
Masson, André, 13
Mercure de France, 49
Millais, Sir John Everett, 13, 74, *76–77*
Le Mirliton, 45
Miró, Joan, 13
Le Miroir, 8, 17, 19
Modersohn-Becker, Paula, 14
Monet, Claude, 8, *28–30*
Morisot, Berthe, 14

Le Nain jaune, 17
Narrenschiff, 89
Nast, Thomas, 13
Neue Jugend, 13
Neue Sachlichkeit, 100
New Masses, 13, 111, 116
New York Daily News, 111
New Yorker, 8, 13, 14, 69, 111
New York Evening Post, 111
New York Herald, 111
NIB, 45

Oberlander, Adolph, 12

La Paix, 53
Pan, 49
Papitu, 69
Paris Illustré, 45
Pascin, 13, 15, 55, *94–95*, 97
Père Peinard, 12, 24, 37, 38
Philadelphia Inquirer, 101
Philadelphia Press, 101
Picasso, Pablo, 8, 13, 14, 58, 62, *63–67*
Pissarro, Camille, 11, 12, *24–25*, 31, 36, 43, 87
Pissarro, Lucien, 11, 24, 43
Die Pleite, 98
La Plume, 22, 24, 31
PM, 116
Psst!, 36, 38
Puck, 13
Punch, 10–11, 24, 77, 87
Puvis de Chavannes, Pierre Cécile, *20–23*, 83

Der Querschnitt, 13
le Quotidien, 49

le Rabelais, 58
Régamey, Félix, 13
Regnault, Alexandre, 13
Reinhardt, Ad, *114–118*
Réligions, 53
La Révolte, 24, 25, 43
La Revue Blanche, 46, 49, 58, 85
Le Rire, 12, 13, 22, 41, 45, 46, 49, 50, 53, 58, 61, 69
Robinson, Boardman, 13
Rossetti, Dante Gabriel, 8, 13, *74–75*
Die Röte Erde, 13
Rouault, Georges, 14
Rousseau, Henri, 13
Rowlandson, Thomas, 9, 17, 19
Rysselberghe, Théo van, 12

Seurat, Georges, 21, 44
Shahn, Ben, *112–113*
Sickert, Walter Richard, 13, *86–87*
Signac, Paul, 12, *43–44*
La Silhouette, 11
Simplicissimus, 13, 14, 69, *94–95*
Slevogt, Max, 14
Sloan, John, 8, 13, *101–103*, 105, 107
Socialist Call, 101
Le Sourire, 31–32
Steinberg, Saul, 15
Steinlen, T. A., 12, 13, 55, 63

Le Témoin, 69, 90, 93
Les Temps Nouveaux, 12, 13, 24, 37, 38, 43, 44, 53, 58, 59
Thony, Wilhelm, 13
Tiepolo, G. D., 9
Tissot, James Jacques Joseph, 8, 15, *80–81*
Töpffer, Rodolphe, 10
Toulouse-Lautrec, Henri de, 8, 12, 21, 35, 40, *45–47*, 49, 55, 63, 69

ULK, 13, 89, 97

La Vache Enragée, 45
Vallotton, Félix, 9, 11, *48–51*
van Dongen, Kees, 9, 11, 37, *58–59*
van Gogh, Vincent, 40, 63
Vanity Fair, 80–81, 87
Veber, Jean, 13
Vernet, Horace, 13
La Vie en Rose, 13
La Vie Moderne, 37
La Vie Parisienne, 61
Villon, Jacques, 8, 9, 12, 45, *55–57*
Vuillard, Edouard, 49

Westermann, H. C., 13
Whistler, James, 14, 87
Willette, Adolphe, 12, 13